Men speak out to Helen Smith, PhD

"I just don't think girls respect guys anymore."
–Blake, Twenty-Seven, White, Physical Therapy Assistant

"I think the danger of life, for men, is failure."
–Max, Twenty-One, White, Student

"If you love freedom, you are now an extremist."
–Max, Twenty-One, White, Student

"Women use the government as the authority, instead of
a man in the house, now that they don't have one."
–Ben, Twenty-One, White, Student

"American men are too tolerant, and it's going to kill them."
–Navid, Fifty, Iranian-American, Entrepreneur

"I've never met a drug dealer or violent
man that was short of women."
–Bradley, Forty-Five, Cuban-Jewish, Nutritionist

"My brother drank himself to death [...] he
basically married the same woman I did."
–Charlie, Fifty-Two, White, CEO

"We have to write our own narrative."
–Kenneth, Forty-Seven, Black, Massage Therapist

"I like myself, and I'm not changing who I am
and what I value in order to be married."
–Randy, Fifty-Seven, Black, Personal Trainer

"Feminism is about what is convenient for her."
–Wyatt, Fifty-Six, White, Engineer

"One bad date asked me if I was a misogynist."
–Wyatt, Fifty-Six, White, Engineer

"Find an outlier if you want to be happy."
–Jack, Seventy, White, Writer

"Find a woman you would take a bullet for."
–Sergio, Seventy-Three, Armenian-American, Physician

"It's the media who is trying to divide men and women."
–Kenneth, Forty-Seven, Black, Massage Therapist

"It's up to us to say to women, 'I hear you
and I want to understand you, but I need
you to hear me and understand me.'"
–Kenneth, Forty-Seven, Black, Massage Therapist

"If you are 21–25, you can go to a bar, but it is not my
scene. How do you meet someone in your thirties now?"
–Preston, Thirty-One, White, Digital Media Consultant

HIS
SIDE

MEN SPEAK OUT
ON DATING, MARRIAGE,
AND LIFE IN AMERICA

HELEN SMITH, PhD

BOMBARDIER
BOOKS

Published by Bombardier Books
An Imprint of Post Hill Press
ISBN: 979-8-89565-358-6
ISBN (eBook): 979-8-89565-359-3

His Side:
Men Speak Out on Dating, Marriage, and Life in America
© 2026 by Helen Smith, PhD
All Rights Reserved

Cover Design by Conroy Accord

Post Hill Press
New York • Nashville
posthillpress.com

Published in the United States of America
1 2 3 4 5 6 7 8 9 10

To my parents who allowed me to fly,
and to Glenn and Julia who just get me.
And to the amazing men who gave me the
opportunity to hear them, thank you.

TABLE OF CONTENTS

"Average men are the beating board of our era."
Forty-five-year-old Bradley from Queens

E veryone says that men won't talk about their thoughts and their feelings. That's wrong. Men are happy to talk, when they feel they'll be listened to, and when they don't think they'll be abused or mocked for what they say. And they do. They've talked to me. Their voices have helped me understand the problems men face in the current female-centered society, and have given me ideas on how to help men help themselves get to a better place.

I think about my privilege as a woman in this society on a daily basis. If this sounds odd to you, hear me out. As a woman, I walk around freely without people thinking I am a pervert for smiling at their kid, out to hurt them or as a symbol of toxic patriarchy. I can express emotions more readily without condemnation and no one denigrates my sex on a daily basis without blowback. Women go to college more often, are more likely to have health insurance,[1] get custody of children the majority of the time, and hold the legal cards when it comes to dating, marriage and long-term relationships. And this is just the tip of the iceberg; the first chapter of this book will describe in more detail the issues that men deal with just for the sin of having been born with an XY chromosome. It is my female privilege that allows me to write about this topic in a way that most men can't.

Men are said to hold the privilege in this country but this book will explode that claim. Norah Vincent who wrote the book *Self-Made Man,*[2] went undercover as a man for eighteen months and found out that it was women who held privilege, not necessarily men. "Ironically, Vincent said, it took experiencing life as a man for her to appreciate being a woman. 'I really like being a woman.... I like it more now because I think it's more of a privilege.'"[3]

Most men in America accept the fact that they are often treated as second-class citizens without questioning what is happening and why. Or they understand it and feel nothing can be done—the system is stacked against them. Other men are successful and doing well but realize that being male comes with risks, both psychological and physical, that most women will never endure nor understand. Even men today who have good marriages and solid careers know that their good fortune can change in a New York minute.

---

[1] "Mars vs. Venus: The gender gap in health," *Harvard Health Publishing*, August 26, 2019. https://www.health.harvard.edu/newsletter_article/mars-vs-venus-the-gender-gap-in-health

[2] Norah Vincent, *Self-Made Man: One Woman's Journey into Manhood and Back Again* (Viking, New York, January 19, 2006).

[3] "A Self-Made Man," ABC News, January 20, 2006. https://abcnews.go.com/2020/Entertainment/story?id=1526982

These are the smart men but there are other men who have no idea how the average man in America feels, what he deals with and how he copes, nor do they care. If some awareness creeps through, they quickly dismiss their fellow man as a whiner or loser. I hope this book can change these men's minds but more importantly, this book is for the so-called average man who is on the front lines in a country that views him with contempt if not downright hostility. Women's needs are put first and the culture is female-focused. How does this knowledge affect the average guy? How are they living their lives knowing that men are living in a society geared to the needs of women? And more importantly, how do men value and keep ahold of their masculinity in the current feminine milieu, and lead a successful life despite the political and societal changes that advantage women over men?

If a man dares to voice an opinion, no matter how reasonable, about men's needs or justice, he is treated with contempt, anger and accusations of misogyny. This book gives men the opportunity to share their honest thoughts and feelings about being male in society—something you would think would be routine but isn't. Men's protests were finally heard in the recent election of Donald Trump, who won men's votes with a 10 percent gender gap—54 percent men to 44 percent women.[4]

The 2024 election is over but the issues behind it live on and will affect future elections and, more importantly, daily life. Trump was elected and it was in part this "silent male voter," represented by some of the men that I interviewed that put him

---

[4]   Katharina Buchholz, "The Trump-Harris Gender Gap," *Statista*, November 6, 2024. https://www.statista.com/chart/33408/female-male-us-voters-exit-polls/

in office.[5] Who are these "silent men" and what would they say to us if they had a megaphone? Not all of the men I interviewed supported Trump, and some were liberal or libertarian, but all of them understood that the current political and social environment was one that was *not* welcoming to men and that change was needed. Many of the men were savvy to the fact that women's needs and culture rule the current zeitgeist, especially the younger ones, but were rarely asked for their opinion. It is just a given that men have always had a voice (not true) and that their needs are at the forefront (again, not true).

I went out over the course of a year before the election to find these men and share their voices with readers so you can understand how men in America feel about relationships and life. Believe it or not, no one ever really asks regular men directly how they feel about much, especially when it comes to their personal opinions and internal dialogue about love and life as a man. We hear *her* side all the time, but what about *his*? Every man I interviewed ended up talking the entire time and willingly showed up eager to share their views. Why is that? Because it is so rare that anyone wants to hear what men really think and feel.

Her side about men and social issues is everywhere—in the news, on social media, and in books and women's studies classes. There is almost nothing women can't say about men (with no repercussions) and to call them on it is met with anger, entitlement and ostracism. Case in point: There is a Facebook page called, "Are We Dating The Same Guy?" The description is, "A place where women can speak freely, openly and honestly

---

5   Claire Lehmann, "Revenge of the Silent Male Voter," *Quillette*, November 6, 2024. https://quillette.com/2024/11/06/the-revenge-of-the-silent-male-voter-trump-vance-musk/

without the fear of harassment or intimidation." Women can freely post pictures of their boyfriend and ask other women if they are dating him and then out him if another woman says she is. Even the women reading these boards state that they contain catty, mean-spirited comments and often untruths about the men on display. Some of the women even make anonymous allegations of domestic violence or rape.[6] There are over 150,000 members in the New York group alone.[7]

Where can a man go to speak freely, openly and honestly without fear of harassment or intimidation? Not very many places. Even Facebook's Mark Zuckerberg was targeted for discussing "toxic masculinity" on Joe Rogan's podcast.[8] All he said was that diversity, equity and inclusion (DEI) programs have "culturally neutered" corporate America.[9] It certainly has and the men I talked to confirmed that for me. If Zuckerberg can't talk freely (kind of ironic—given the censorship of Facebook) imagine what happens to men who don't own a billion-dollar business. If they dare speak openly on chat boards, most of men's voices are reinterpreted by feminist men or women as misogynistic, false or damaged. Or worse, groups like "Diverting Hate" get $700,000 in grant money from the Department of Homeland Security to go after men who dare

---

6   Amy Eileen Hamm, "Are We Dating the same Guy?" *Quillette*, September 21, 2023. https://quillette.com/2023/09/21/are-we-dating-the-same-guy/
7   See https://www.facebook.com/groups/340985311306448/
8   Ariel Zilber, "Bay Area lawyer drops Meta as client over CEO Mark Zuckerberg's 'toxic masculinity and Neo-Nazi madness'," *New York Post*, January 15, 2025. https://nypost.com/2025/01/15/business/lawyer-drops-meta-over-ceo-mark-zuckerbergs-neo-nazi-madness/
9   Rachel Wolf, "Mark Zuckerberg praises benefits of 'masculine energy,' says DEI 'culturally neutered' corporate America," *New York Post*, January 11, 2025. https://nypost.com/2025/01/11/business/mark-zuckerberg-praises-benefits-of-masculine-energy-says-dei-culturally-neutered-corporate-america/

say anything negative about women even if it's true.[10] Who wants to be targeted by a government funded agency even if it purports to "help" men? This is not the kind of help men need.

Books on men are often not much better, being generally derogatory or smug. I was recently at Barnes & Noble and right up front was a book written by a feminist author about men whose PR blurb read "Because if men have neither learned to mine their deepest anxieties about masculinity for comedy, nor answered the question "What About Men?," then it's up to a busy woman to do it."[11] This snark alone is enough to infer that the author has no idea how men feel with the slings they receive on a daily basis. She is just placating her female audience with how empowered and put upon women are. And her title *What about Men?: A Feminist Answers the Question*[12] is enough to give one pause about her motives—it is to help women, not men. She seems to have little understanding of how men really feel; they are alien to her, and not even real people. Apparently, she is on "Team Tits" but needs to dig into the man question so her teenage daughters and others like them can be happy. Men are an afterthought.

Women and society interpret what they think men feel and think without asking them for their own words or if they do,

[10] "How the Department of Homeland Security Wasted $700,000 in Taxpayer Money on "Diverting Hate," May 2, 2024. https://captaincapitalism.blogspot.com/search?q="How+the+Department+of+Homeland+Security+Wasted+percent24700percent2C000+in+Taxpayer+Money+on+"Diverting+Hatepercent2C"+

See also https://drive.google.com/file/d/1-i_NeesyWl_p7blfVLAYBdhk n05bjCHQ/view?pli=1 for a copy of the report.

[11] Caitlin Moran, *What about Men: A Feminist Answers the Question* (Harper Perennial, New York, September, 2023). https://www.harpercollins.com/products/what-about-men-caitlin-moran?variant=41364865810466

[12] Caitlin Moran, *What about Men: A Feminist Answers the Question* (Harper Perennial, New York, September, 2023).

they twist them to make men fit a narrative that is generally negative. How is this going to help men lead better lives? *His Side*, in contrast, strives to put men's unfiltered and honest voices on its pages so that other men (and concerned women) can learn and understand firsthand how men are feeling right now about dating, marriage and life in America. More importantly, what are the steps individual men and society can take to help men lead better lives?

When people hear you are writing a book on men, most of them think it will be a self-help book to help *women* deal with the problem man in their life. I was at a nail salon one day when the manicurist asked me what kind of book I was writing. Once I mentioned it was on men, the women in the salon chimed in. "Why do men only give 25 percent?" one woman asked. "Maybe because they think women only give 10 percent," I said. "Oh, I have someone to send you," others would say, though what they usually mean is "this guy is a problem for me and I want someone to fix him." Or I am told, "Men don't know how to express themselves, they are not verbally astute, they don't understand their emotions."

Actually, men do talk when they feel someone is listening. But the truth is, almost no one really cares deep down how men *really* feel and if men do speak out, most people don't like it or accept it or even understand it. And, it is not just women who don't understand. When men hear or see other men complain, they often call them "whiners." It's no wonder men rarely talk freely about how they feel—even their own cohorts may treat them like pariahs or losers.

This book demonstrates that men have a lot to say and their views are just as valid as women's. You may not like what you hear, or you may agree with it, but I have asked men at different stages and ages to tell me about themselves, their feelings and their opinions about how their lives are going. They were real and honest. I found their responses fascinating. I hope you do too.

So why is a woman writing about men? It depends on who you ask. According to the Southern Poverty Law Center (SPLC), any discussion of men's rights or needs means that one is engaged with some kind of twisted misogynistic group of white supremacists. The SPLC had an alarming article about how any woman who stands up for men, such as myself or author Christina Hoff Sommers, who wrote *The War Against Boys,* are tools who lend an "air of respectability" to these groups.[13] Thanks for the compliment, I guess, but I find this take kind of funny because it is not at all true. It's not surprising though because many of the accusations this group makes are self-serving and not based on actual facts. SPLC is mainly hustling for cash by announcing anyone they disagree with is a hate group,[14] but enough about them. My interest is in helping men lead better lives. If that makes me a gender traitor, so be it.

The real reason I am interested in men and their lives is because as a psychologist and fellow human being, I believe that men deserve justice and the pursuit of happiness just as women do. I have been passionate about men's issues since grad school when my first client as a psychology intern was a wheelchair bound man who was being beaten by his wife. With nowhere

---

[13] Tyler O'Neil, "SPLC Slams 'Factual Feminist' and Other Women as Part of 'Male Supremacy' Movement," *PJ Media,* February 25, 2018. https://pjmedia.com/tyler-o-neil/2018/02/25/splc-slams-factual-feminist-and-other-women-as-male-supremacists-n56465#google_vignette

[14] Kyle Smith, "Hate, Inc.: The SPLC Is a Hyper-Partisan Scam," *National Review,* March 1, 2018. https://www.nationalreview.com/2018/03/southern-poverty-law-center-bias-hate-group-labels-scam/

to go for resources for my client, there was not much that could be done. After all, he was a man and she was a woman, the former an oppressor, the latter the victim. I felt helpless and my client felt even worse. That was over thirty years ago and things have not gotten better for men in our society. I think about this fact every day.

Every time I talk to men about their relationships, their work or their educational opportunities (or lack thereof), the same helpless feeling comes over me that I had with my very first client. I am writing this book because I cannot sit idly by and watch our hostile society destroy masculinity, what writer Camille Paglia called "the most creative cultural force in history."[15]

In response to the political and social issues that men faced, I wrote the book *Men on Strike: Why Men are Boycotting Marriage, Fatherhood and the American Dream—and Why it Matters* over ten years ago. In that book, I described those issues—from a lack of rights in marriage and reproduction to the decline of male spaces to a dearth of due process at colleges. Many men across the country wrote me to say the book had helped them understand the problems associated with being male in the twenty-first century. But understanding the problems isn't enough. It is also important to have the tools to deal with the psychological and emotional upheaval brought about by classifying men as the problem and female-centered solutions as the answer. However, *Men on Strike* was a call to action and an explanation of what was happening to men in twenty-first century America and though it did offer some advice and solutions, this book picks up on that theme and expands it with

---

[15] Camile Paglia, "Perspective Needed—Feminism's Lie: Denying Reality About Sexual Power And Rape," *Seattle Times*, February 17, 1991.

men's actual voices telling first-person accounts of what they are dealing with in the ever changing gender wars. What is the state of mind of the American male today? How are they coping and dealing with the changing gender dynamics, dating, marriage and life circumstances for today's guy?

A book like this is necessary because so many experts miss the point, believing that men are retreating from society or that they're not living up to their full potential due to fear, laziness, lack of motivation and male privilege. It may look that way on the surface, but if experts would listen with an open mind to what men actually say they would find that something very different is actually going on.

My goal is not to tell men that they are falling short, but to explain the changes that have come about that make men's purpose and goals more difficult to reach today than in the past. We live in a knowledge-based society, dominated by a service industry that favors women and their skill sets.

This is not by accident, but by design. The current situation is a political one that discriminates against men, especially white men but others as well. This discrimination has seeped into every aspect of culture. Take for example, how even traditional churches have become female-focused with groups, conferences and congregations on women's concerns but not much for men. Many of the churches have "gone woke" and have left men to find other alternatives. Wisely, men are turning away from traditional churches and reaching out to more orthodox ones that are not afraid of masculinity.[16]

---

[16] Susie Coen, "Young, single men are leaving traditional churches. They found a more 'masculine' alternative," *The Telegraph*, January 4, 2025. https://www.telegraph.co.uk/us/news/2025/01/04/the-young-men-leaving-traditional-churches-for-orthodox/

This is just one example of how masculinity is viewed as inconsequential, dangerous or toxic or just politically incorrect. Most young men and even older ones have no idea what masculinity even looks like, nor have they learned why it is important. It is hard to define the problem of men if many young men (and older ones) today do not know what masculinity looks like. Most younger guys have been indoctrinated since birth to view their lives and American culture without a focus on real masculinity but through the lens of "toxic masculinity" or no masculinity at all. (Most young men probably seldom hear the word "masculinity" without "toxic" coming before it.) Downplaying true masculinity results in confusion at best and a life of depression and malaise at worse. This lack of knowledge is a political and societal maneuver to neuter average men and keep them silent and afraid to stand up for their rights and needs. Alternatively, some men, in a sort of Stockholm syndrome, are indoctrinated to believe that the only needs that matter are those of women, or they get political or social gains from going along with discrimination against their own sex. Either way, it is imperative that this cycle be broken so that the average man in America can lead a better life.

In his book, *Manhood: The Masculine Virtues America Needs*, Senator Josh Hawley described working as a law professor and realizing that for one of his male students, "John," the prospect of living as an independent man paralyzed him and with that paralysis came a deep sense of shame. "He was failing as a man before he had even begun."[17] Many men feel like "John" but why? What does it mean to be a man? What are the goals of men? Hawley has his own ideas of what these

---

[17]   Josh Hawley, *Manhood: The Masculine Virtues America Needs* (Regnery, New York, 2023), 4.

manly virtues are, which I will discuss in the next chapter. However, my focus is the purposes and goals I heard directly from the men I spent time interviewing, to describe what men themselves find important. Masculinity may mean something different to individual men but from what I can gather, men who believe that masculinity is important have a common set of goals and values in their lives that I will refer to later as the themes leading to happiness and success for men.

Those themes were discussed by the men I interviewed and seemed to boil down to purpose—helping a family or society, being a good father, and husband, finding meaningful work that pays the bills and supports themselves or their family. They were less likely than women to want government intervention into their lives and wanted to be autonomous—to sink or swim based on their own idea and pursuit of what would bring them and their families happiness. Some of the men believed strongly in merit and were against diversity, inclusion and equity (DEI) that limited their ability to rise in an organization or in life. They saw risk-taking as important and many mentioned that a man's role was to provide for and help their families. All of them wanted to have good relationships with women and respected and admired their qualities.

All of them loved women, even if they had been disappointed by them in the past. But just as important, or maybe more so for some of the men, relationships with other men, from fathers to teachers to friends, were paramount, and often missing. This lack of positive male role models (and the presence of some negative ones) led to challenges in later life. Many of those were overcome, but some wounds were obviously still with these men. Many young men today look for role models that understand what it is to be a man in America. Even hugely successful men like Elon Musk understand how important having an American dream is for men.[18] Many young men are inspired by Musk who understands that purpose and masculinity are intertwined.

I went out to find these men and talk to them about living in America and what it means to be a man who is dating, married or engaged in life in the US. The men were heterosexual, from a variety of demographics and backgrounds. Where did I find these men? Interviewees were referred to me by friends, acquaintances, by asking on podcasts for men willing to be interviewed, and by reaching out to men online. Sometimes, I asked men who I thought would be good interviews if they would be willing to talk. All but one or two were happy to be interviewed, but all the men I asked agreed. I asked each one of them to honestly speak out on dating, marriage, and life in general or any of their concerns about living as a male in America. This is not to say that men in other countries don't have concerns, but this book is focused on men living in the US (although one interviewee was foreign-born and many others were first- or second-generation Americans).

I interviewed the men by age, starting with the younger age groups from twenty-one to thirty-four, including a group of fraternity guys, then moved on to talking with middle-aged men, and finally with men over fifty-five (who, yes, are still middle-aged) but I wanted their perspective to contrast with younger guys. The interviews took place at the men's jobs, the closest Starbucks, diners, my office or by Zoom. The fraternity

---

[18] Tim Higgins, "On the Campaign Trail With Elon Musk: Offering Young Men an American Dream," *The Wall Street Journal*, October 18, 2024. https://www.wsj.com/tech/on-the-campaign-trail-with-elon-musk-offering-young-men-an-american-dream-05bd0349?st=JS3GNM&reflink=article_imessage_share

men even let me come to their frat house and interview a bunch of guys at once. I always taped their sessions and took notes so I could make sure I understood what they were telling me. I often followed up in person or by email to get more information. I wanted to talk to men in places where they felt comfortable and could open up about their experiences without outside interference.

All of these men were doing fairly well in society and I asked them for advice and ideas for other men who might still need help. With their answers and insight, maybe their voices can help other men learn how to survive and thrive in this female-focused society that has lost sight of how important men are to everyone. But before turning to the men's own words, let's start by tackling some of the most important issues facing men today in the next chapter.

H.S.
Knoxville, Tennessee 2025

CHAPTER ONE

How the Female-Centric Culture Harms Men and Boys

"There is no such thing as toxic masculinity. There is only masculinity and the aspects of it that conflict with, or benefit, women in a female-centered society."
Rollo Tomassi, author of The Rational Male[19]

"Everything now is seen through the lens of women."
Forty-five-year-old interviewee from Queens, New York

Female-centricity is alive and well in our culture, even before a child is born. Dads-to-be are now twice as likely to want

---

19 Rollo Tomassi, *The Rational Male* (CreateSpace Independent Publishing Platform, 2013). https://twitter.com/RationalMale/status/16030814604366 80704?lang=en

Rollo Tomassi (@RationalMale), "There is no such thing as toxic masculinity...." X, December 14, 2022, https://x.com/RationalMale/status/ 1603081460436680704 their firstborn child to be a girl as they used to be, and mothers are 24 percent more likely to prefer a girl.[20] I heard this prejudice against boys firsthand when a pregnant waitress told me she hoped she would have a girl because there were "too many boys in the world." Really? It doesn't seem like we are overrun with men these days, especially in the educational and health systems.

And after birth, this scarcity of men only gets worse. Young boys are dropped off at kindergarten where their chance of meeting a male teacher is probably lower than of getting killed by a terrorist. This comes from an old *Newsweek* article from the 1980's that had a troubling punchline stating that a woman over 40 was "more likely to be killed by terrorism" than to ever marry.[21] Now the odds of a five-year-old boy seeing a male face as he goes about his day are low. In the United States, "91.8% of all kindergarten teachers are women, while 8.2% are men."[22] There is even a meme going around the internet noting the irony of "toxic masculinity" that correctly states:

> *"43% of boys are raised by single mothers. 78% of teachers are female.*
>
> *So, close to 50% of boys have 100% feminine influence while at home & an 8/10ish chance of 100% feminine influence at school. Toxic*

---

[20] Warren Farrell and John Gray, *The Boy Crisis: Why Our Boys Are Struggling and What We Can Do About It* (BenBella Books, Inc., Dallas, 2018), 2.

[21] Megan Garber, "When *Newsweek* Struck Terror in the Hearts of Single Women,'" *The Atlantic*, June 2016. https://www.theatlantic.com/entertainment/archive/2016/06/more-likely-to-be-killed-by-a-terrorist-than-to-get-married/485171/

[22] "Kindergarten Teacher Demographics and Statistics In The US," *Zippia*. https://www.zippia.com/kindergarten-teacher-jobs/demographics/

masculinity isn't the problem. The lack of masculinity is. "[23]

Given the lack of fathers in our society and the lack of male role models, it is no wonder that boys are left to make up their own version of manhood or to incorporate the media version that tells them they are defective girls or worse. Masculinity is viewed as unclear and undesirable, and men are not doing as well in many areas of life as they used to be. Many experts believe men and boys are in crisis in the modern world and they seek to answer the question of why.

There have been many books and articles written on the topic of "the boy and men crisis" over the past ten years since I wrote *Men on Strike*. (For purposes of this book, I will use the following dictionary definition: a crisis is "a condition of instability or danger, as in social, economic, political, or international affairs, leading to a decisive change."[24]) It seems that these authors each have their own version of why we have this current male crisis but for purposes of this book, I use "crisis" to mean that men in today's political and social climate are often in an unstable or dangerous situation because our culture puts women and girls first and men and boys last. There are other reasons of course, and I will focus on those also.

This women-first focus has inadvertently caused men to lose jobs, stop going to college, lose interest in school, and dwell on relationships with online (or, increasingly, AI) women because they can't find a real woman who finds them acceptable. Why is this happening? Different experts and authors give plausible

---

[23] Miss Stirr (@missstirr), "43% of boys are raised by single mothers," X, August 9, 2018. https://twitter.com/missstirr/status/1027412051218636802?lang=en

[24] "Crisis, Definition and Meaning," Dictionary.com. https://www.dictionary.com/browse/crisis

accounts of why men are not "measuring up" or why they are in "crisis." I have scoured scores of books over the years but the following are the ones I think are important in understanding what's going on with men's own lives in the later chapters.

The books I read were good and addressed certain aspects of what is furthering this crisis but none of them (at least in my opinion) really gets at the full picture of how we got here, what are the causes, and more importantly, how men can improve their lives with the information. Each book is a piece of the puzzle in explaining the "crisis" but doesn't fully explain how men's lives are being affected and what needs to change. I will use the ideas in these books, together with my own views of our women-first society, to illustrate why men are changing the way they interact in society—and how they are coping successfully (or not) with these changes.

In this section, I will provide you with a summary of some of the books I found most important, what ideas were most salient, and finally, in later chapters show examples of how these ideas play out in the lives of the men that I personally interviewed. Let's turn first to the most influential of the male crisis books to put the men's voices in perspective.

Purpose

"For certain young men in Pennsylvania and elsewhere, who feel left behind, that's the new American dream. Purpose. And Musk is showing them that."[25]

---

[25] Tim Higgins, "On the Campaign Trail With Elon Musk: Offering Young Men an American Dream," *The Wall Street Journal*, October 18, 2024. https://www.wsj.com/tech/on-the-campaign-trail-with-elon-musk-offering-young-men-an-american-dream-05bd0349?st=JS3GNM&reflink=article_imessage_share

My favorite book is *The Boy Crisis* written by Warren Farrell and John Gray. This is a long treatise of 496 pages that is an excellent read for someone who truly wants to understand the psychology and summary of the challenges facing boys in this country. I know because I read it when it came out in order to write an endorsement for it. The main takeaway of the book is that dads and men are no longer as available in the lives of boys and that this, along with other structural and societal changes, results in boys feeling purposeless and lost. Masculinity used to come with a sense of purpose, of being the protector and provider (for example, warrior, sole breadwinner). Today, there is a purpose void.[26] I agree completely that boys need dads and men in their lives. But the solution for the authors is for men to become a "new kind of man." The authors seem to boil down this new man to one who acts on his feelings and is empathetic. "Women will increasingly want your son to also have emotional and relationship intelligence," the authors emphasize.[27] In other words, the solution is for men to become more like women or at least kind of androgynous in order to fit into this new world or at least to get a girlfriend. Is this good advice? Honestly, the more emotionally equipped men are not always the most successful with women. As one of my interviewees pointed out—the most undesirable men often end up with the most women. "I've never met a drug dealer or violent man that was short of women," he said. The truth is, emotional intelligence is important but there are other kinds of emotional intelligence than woman's empathy which may or may not be healthy.

---

[26] Warren Farrell and John Gray, *The Boy Crisis: Why Our Boys Are Struggling and What We Can Do About It* (BenBella Books, Inc., Dallas, 2018), 82.

[27] Id. at p 82

Learning to be empathetic in the same way as women is not the answer for many men who would not be happy with the emotions that our society says women possess—nor would the women honestly. The new heroic intelligence, according to the theme of the book, is one that leads with emotional and health intelligence. Ultimately, the conclusion the authors reach is one of gender liberation which is to free the sexes from rigid roles. So rather than being protectors or breadwinners in the traditional sense, the authors feel the solution to the crisis is for men to break free from these traditional roles. As you will see in the following interviews I did with men, this protector and breadwinner role is not easily shed, either by a man himself or by the women he dates or marries. And if he sheds these roles because society and research tell him to, will he be happy or even stay married? How much of this unhappiness is caused by denigrating the traits of traditional men? Maybe society needs to learn to value these traits again.

Many men feel that their purpose is to help, provide, and protect and that to denigrate or deny these feelings is no different than denying women their feelings of femininity or nurturing. To be clear, I myself am not much into gender roles, but that doesn't mean that men or women who feel differently should have to change who they are to suit me. Society should not denigrate men for valuing traditional masculine traits. They are valuable and rewarding to society and to the men themselves.

To be clear, Farrell and Gray's book does not denigrate male traits, it seeks to find ways for men to use them in more emotional or helpful ways and to expand their options outside of provider and breadwinner. However, I believe that masculine men who want to be traditional should also be valued, and the traits men possess should also be seen as valuable.

The book does, however, provide a great service by pointing out the research on dads and how important they are. The data in the book are of utmost importance, showing for example, that boys who suffer from father-loss have, by the age of nine, a 14 percent reduction in life expectancy as predicted by shorter telomeres. Boys are also far more likely than girls to do poorly in a single-mother family, especially in families of divorce, and finally, boys are likely to fare worse than girls when moving to a new neighborhood, even a better one. This is due to boys "vulnerability when losing old friendships and because their less developed social skills leave them more challenged in creating new ones."[28] This research held true when I talked to guys who lost fathers due to divorce or death, as you will read about in later chapters.

The next book I picked up with a similar theme of "why can't men become more like women" was by Richard V. Reeves, a senior fellow in economic studies at the Brookings Institution, entitled *Of Boys and Men: Why the Modern Male is Struggling, Why It Matters and What to Do About It.*[29] My daughter had read it a while back and thought I would like it and I did, though I waited to read it because I was sure it would be elitist in tone, and annoy me. I was not wrong. The tone is elitist and apologetic, as if the author is sorry that he has to say anything positive about boys and men. In fact, he states he was advised not to write the book because "in the current political climate,

---

[28] Warren Farrell and John Gray, *The Boy Crisis: Why Our Boys Are Struggling and What We Can Do About It* (BenBella Books, Inc., Dallas, 2018), 395.

[29] Richard V. Reeves, *Of Boys and Men: Why the Modern Male is Struggling, Why It Matters, and What to Do About it* (Brookings Institution Press, Washington DC, 2022).

highlighting the problems of boys and men is seen as a perilous undertaking."[30] He seems to view himself as a real hero for this undertaking. And maybe he is.

Despite the elitist tone, he does make some very valuable points about part of what is happening with men. After all, he has three sons and studies trends in the economic and structural changes that men face and he is wise enough to admit that what he calls "male malaise" is a problem. He goes into detail in the first chapters of the book describing the changing economic, social and cultural changes that men face. For that, I am grateful. Many people put their heads in the sand and will not even admit that men are facing a different world that is not in their favor. Reeves argues that "the rapid liberation of women and the labor-market shift toward brains and away from brawn have left men bereft of what the sociologist David Morgan calls 'ontological security.' They now confront the prospect of 'cultural redundancy.'"[31]

What does this academic jargon mean? Ontological security means a "purposeful sense of self imbued with meaning."[32] It means that men, like everyone else, like to feel they understand their place in the world and how the world works. For example, if you smile at a woman and are just trying to be nice or even flirt, you don't face the threat of jail or the loss of your job. If you have a job and work hard, you are valued by your

---

[30]   Richard V. Reeves, *Of Boys and Men: Why the Modern Male is Struggling, Why It Matters, and What to Do About it* (Brookings Institution Press, Washington DC, 2022)., Preface, ix.

[31]   Idrees Kahloon, "What's the Matter with Men?," *The New Yorker* book review, January 23, 2023. https://www.newyorker.com/magazine/2023/01/30/whats-the-matter-with-men

[32]   Maggie Phillips, "Richard V. Reeves and Jocko Willink Take on Male Malaise," *wordonfire.org*, March 1, 2024. https://www.wordonfire.org/articles/richard-v-reeves-and-jocko-willink-take-on-male-malaise/

family and society. That was then. Now men are blamed for every ill of the world but still expected to earn a living, provide, protect and never come across as "creepy" and do so without complaining or expecting respect or to be valued. And they are said to be sexist if they mention being a breadwinner.

Cultural redundancy comes from a British term meaning that you are laid off as you are no longer needed. In other words, the culture no longer needs men; they are superfluous, unnecessary. As the feminists say: "A woman without a man is like a fish without a bicycle."[33] Reeves mentions an influential 1980 essay by William Goode who observed that "the underlying shift is toward the decreasing marginal utility of males."[34] Reeves states, "True, but ouch."[35] This is ridiculous. Who is to say that the culture no longer needs men? The elite? Progressives? Others? Who has the right to determine that men are not needed or are irrelevant? When women were not doing as well as men, everyone said it was due to gender discrimination and unfair laws. When men are not doing as well, we're told it is because they are not needed.

My problem with Reeves' position is that he doesn't understand the hostility of a society that views men with such contempt and the impact of this negative view of men on their psyche, even if the men themselves don't realize where the hostility is coming from. He says many things in his book about men that are useful and true, but much of what he says

---

[33] "Quote Origin: A Woman Without a Man is Like a Fish Without a Bicycle," Quote Investigator, October 8, 2016. https://quoteinvestigator.com/2016/10/18/fish-bicycle/

[34] William J. Goode, "Why Men Resist," *Dissent*, (Spring 1980).

[35] Richard V. Reeves, *Of Boys and Men: Why the Modern Male is Struggling, Why It Matters, and What to Do About It* (Brookings Institution Press, Washington DC, 2022), 36.

is marred by the fact that he is so afraid of offending women and so concerned with placating progressive ideologues that he offers few substantive solutions, except for advocating for boys to start school later due to a lack of maturity or for men to go into the healing professions like nursing or teaching just as women have gone into STEM. Reeves writes on his *Substack*, "We need a massive national effort to get men to move into jobs in the growing fields of health, education, administration, and literacy (HEAL), equivalent to the successful campaign to get women into STEM."[36]

The truth is that much of what is happening to men today is a direct result of discrimination and not just the structural changes Reeves describes. In addition, the structural changes are not exactly organic in nature; they are part of a changing elitist globalism that determines who succeeds using credentials and a "knowledge-based" service industry focusing on soft skills and EQ (emotional intelligence). These "skills" favor women more than men. It is not helpful to blame only structural changes without the accompanying discrimination against men that has led to so many of the current problems. Both are possible. Reeves writes that "We can hold two thoughts in our heads at once,"[37] but he should do the same. Or perhaps he is too much a product of his environment to see things clearly when it comes to discrimination against men.

He points out that "In the US, a third of men of all political persuasions believe that they are discriminated against, and among Republicans, the number is rising."[38] Reeves says this

---

[36] Richard V. Reeves, "Men can HEAL," *Substack*, September 25, 2022. https://ofboysandmen.substack.com/p/men-can-heal
[37] Reeves, *Of Boys and Men*,, Print..2022
[38] Reeves, *Of Boys and Men*, 120.

discrimination is *false*. It is not. For example, even the London School of Economics, hardly a bastion of right wing politics, found that female teachers gave lower marks to boys and gave higher grades to girls. In contrast, "girls tend to believe male teachers will look upon them more favourably than female teaching staff, but men treat all students the same, regardless of gender."[39] Note that the girls feel entitled to getting better grades from a man while boys know that a female teacher will ding them for being male. Ninety-seven percent of all alimony is paid by men,[40] yet "the share of women who earn as much as or significantly more than their husbands has roughly tripled"[41] over the last half-century. Men are seen as walking ATM's *because* they are men. Men are denied due process at college even if they are falsely accused of sexual harassment. I can go on and on, but you get the idea. Reeves mentions the failings of our education system but denies any discrimination. Yet boys get better grades at all-boys' schools than when they're in a co-ed school. In fact, boys no longer lag behind girls when they are in single-sex schools.[42] Reeves is not a fan of single-sex

---

[39] Lucy Sherriff, "Female Teachers Give Male Pupils Lower Marks, Claims Study," *Huffington Post*, February 16, 2012. https://www.huffingtonpost.co.uk/2012/02/16/female-teachers-give-male_n_1281236.html

[40] Emma Johnson, " Why Do So Few Men Get Alimony?" *Forbes*, November 20, 2014. https://www.forbes.com/sites/emmajohnson/2014/11/20/why-do-so-few-men-get-alimony/?sh=3b30602954b9

[41] Richard Fry, Carolina Aragão, Kiley Hurst, and Kim Parker, "In a Growing Share of U.S. Marriages, Husbands and Wives Earn About the Same," Pew Research Center, April 13, 2023. https://www.pewresearch.org/social-trends/2023/04/13/in-a-growing-share-of-u-s-marriages-husbands-and-wives-earn-about-the-same/

[42] "Boys get better grades at all-boys schools: study," *Reuters*, August 24, 2009. https://www.reuters.com/article/lifestyle/boys-get-better-grades-at-all-boys-schools-study-idUSTRE57N1DJ/

schools but the men I talked to who went to them felt it was the "best thing that ever happened to them."

Men are absolutely discriminated against, yet Reeves believes the solution to male problems is for boys to start school later so they will be more mature and for men to go into the healing professions such as teaching or nursing. No mention that schools discriminate against boys so why go longer, and has he ever talked to a male nurse or teacher? I have and the stories I hear about being discriminated against for being male in these fields are very real. Men have told me that in the nursing profession, they are routinely given extra duties such as doing the heavy lifting so female staff doesn't have to; plus, they get abused by supervisors, and looked down on by female staff. Male teachers are looked at as suspect by parents as well as bullied or harassed by other (usually female) teachers. If you don't believe me, then believe this study from Skidmore College in a journal published by the American Psychological Association:

> *Male (vs. female) nurses are viewed as more likely to encounter harassment and rejection (Cherry & Deaux, 1978) and report higher levels of workplace bullying (Erikson & Einarsen, 2004). Further, male early elementary educators report experiencing discrimination (Allan, 1993) and are rated as posing a greater safety threat to children, less likable (Moss-Racusin & Johnson, 2016) and less hirable (Kim & Weseley, 2017) than identical women. Thus, evidence reveals that men in HEED [HEED stands for health*

care, early education, and domestic roles] are
likely to encounter gender biases.[43]

To be fair, Reeves points out this bias in a chapter entitled "Men Can HEAL," so it seems he is aware of what sounds like discrimination to me, but apparently men aren't discriminated against in his book. He thinks that there needs to be a national effort with media and marketing campaigns to make nursing and teaching for men seem "masculine appropriate." But until he gets politicians, women and even other men to stop the psychological and political warfare against the average man, nothing will change. Men do not want a non-traditional job that leads to divorce, ridicule and harassment by women and others. (Would you?) They want respect and a feeling that they matter. If you want to better engage men in non-traditional pursuits or in school or society in general, you also have to change the discrimination and negative attitudes towards men that women and society hold while simultaneously stating men are "privileged."

The next book I picked up was full of respect for men though it is more of the white knight flavor.[44] Senator Josh Hawley's book *Manhood* asks the question, "What makes a man?"[45] I found this book to be a more enjoyable read given

---

[43] Corinne A. Moss-Racusin , Samantha A. Rapp, et.al., "Gender Equality Eliminates Gender Gaps in Engagement With Female-Stereotypic Domains," *Journal of Experimental Psychology: Applied,* 2022. https://www.apa.org/pubs/journals/releases/xap-xap0000459.pdf

[44] A White Knight is a man who wants to take care of women and sees her as a "damsel in distress." Hawley states that men should be providers and protectors, though he doesn't acknowledge that marriage now is a legal minefield for men and that women's standards for men are sometimes impossible.

[45] Hawley, *Manhood*, print. 2023.

that Hawley does not apologize for men and thinks well of masculine qualities.

Hawley's book, in contrast to the Reeves' book, is not fearful in the least and he is straightforward in his thinking. He celebrates manhood in all its glory and looks at what gives men's life purpose and meaning. Though he draws on ancient wisdom from the Greeks and Romans and from the Bible, much of it is pertinent to what is happening today. Masculinity is now viewed as toxic and something to be destroyed. *Manhood* takes the position that the virtues of men such as courage, purpose, character and helping the world become what it was meant to be, matter. That men's work and lives matter. That is a big lesson in a society that tells us that men's lives are trash, that they are responsible for the ills of the world.

For the positive attributes of masculinity, I applaud him. However, much of what Hawley proposes, such as duty, honor, and bravery require some degree of cooperation from others. He says to choose a giant issue in your life, like marriage and run towards it, not away. "Take the risk and injury and pain," he states. "But the willingness to commit, to put everything at risk, is central to what a man is."[46]

But my thoughts are that if a man wants to make his marriage work and he has an unwilling partner, he cannot beat a dead horse and keep trying with a woman who does not want the same, or who threatens him with divorce or blackmail if kids are involved. If a man wants the country to be less dependent on the government and more free, but many citizens reject freedom and use victimhood to silence others, at what point do you keep trying with people who are this entitled and

---

[46] Hawley, *Manhood*, 78.

Machiavellian? At what point does "commitment and risk" become enabling and self-destructive? One of the men I interviewed later in this book did just what Hawley suggests in his marriage and almost ended up in jail. No thanks.

Though it has its flaws, Hawley's book does get the reader to think about what it means to be a man in our society, and it has a positive message about men which is reason enough to read it. However, it does not discuss the changes in the current culture that leave men bewildered and coping with power plays used by society against them that are both personal and political. These power plays can be personal ones, such as those found in dating. For more understanding about the current dating aspects for men, especially for younger men, I turned to a book by Myron Gaines (and edited by Aaron Clarey). This book, like Hawley's book, values men's traits and does not seek to change them but instead, seeks to warn average men that women may not like them that much. It is a bit nihilistic but much of it sounded like what I heard from the younger men in the next chapter.

Mr. Gaines' book, *Why Women Deserve Less*,[47] is at first glance a short polemic on how women use their looks and social media to lure men into being fleeced for profit or tolerated until someone better comes along. Yet, after reading the eighty-six-page book three times (maybe four), I realized it was a masterpiece in the psychological understanding of what is happening in today's online dating scene. I spoke to the editor of the book and he stated that they were aiming it toward young men who like shorter to-the-point books which, is genius on their part. According to Gaines, modern intersexual dynamics

---

[47] Myron Gaines (edited by Aaron Clarey), *Why Women Deserve Less* (Independently published, 2023).

have brought a new normal in how men and women treat each other. He implores men to figure out how these dynamics have changed in order to lead a better life and to avoid failing at relationships again and again. Though the book is a bit harsh, it does have some important kernels of truth that are important for men to understand when dating today, particularly online. In a nutshell, according to Gaines, under the "Old Contract" men and women had with each other, "Men provided resources and protection. Women provided sex (and, if wanted, children)."[48] Feminism has burned this "Old Contract."

Now there is a "New Contract" that boils down to "I don't need a man! Men are trash! Down With the patriarchy! Believe all Women!"[49] In addition, the new contract says that women are "to support themselves independently, requiring no support or subsidy from men. While they, in turn, are no longer needed to provide men with sex, love, support or family."[50] Gaines says that (some, but not all) women have violated the new contract through working less than men, resorting to the government for a higher standard of living (especially single women), negotiating in bad faith by using the internet and dating to extract resources from men, and using victim status and preferential treatment to get advantages in society. Gaines discusses how the internet and Instagram have made it harder for the average man to find the average woman. Women get hundreds of likes and messages a day from men, leading them to feel that they are entitled to the top 1 percent of men (six feet or taller, making 100k plus per year, and physically fit). "The internet

---

[48]   Gaines, pg. 12.
[49]   Myron Gaines (edited by Aaron Clarey), *Why Women Deserve Less* (Independently published, 2023).,pg.12.
[50]   Gaines, *Why Women Deserve Less,* 35.

and the unlimited amount of choice it has given women today has effectively removed most women's interest in most men and also spoiled women to the point they're no longer capable of forming bonding, loving, and committed relationships."[51] It has also made women pickier than ever.

Gaines does not feel that women like most men very much and gives examples such as the famous OK Cupid study where women rated 80 percent of men as unattractive.[52] He states that women still like men, just top-tier ones. In the past your average man could pair up with your average woman but now the internet, especially Instagram, has made that impossible. Women are told they are beautiful constantly, bombarded by messages from men in their inboxes and believe they are entitled to only the best men, even if they themselves lack any of the qualities and looks they desire in their dates. Young men face an environment that has made it almost impossible to find a quality woman. Gaines tells men to improve themselves for their own sake, but if they want a woman, he states, "It's YOUR job to get into the top percentile of men they DO like, not cry about it."[53]

Here I disagree with Gaines, in that he is asking the average man to get to the top 1 percent of men or at least the top 10 percent. There are plenty of good men out there who would make great boyfriends, husbands, and fathers who are not only overlooked but are now being told that they must become the man that *women* want them to be or end up alone. Can't a man be himself and also find a woman who likes him? Must a guy always be involved in some type of power play with women?

[51] Gaines, *Why Women Deserve Less*, 30.
[52] *Gaines, Why Women Deserve Less*, 26.
[53] Gaines, *Why Women Deserve Less*, 33.

I set out to ask men these questions and more to get insight into how men feel about the current state of being a man in today's America.

And I found out that the answers to the questions above were both "yes" and "no." A man can't be himself if he is average and decent, and can be if he was antisocial or a drug dealer. Many of the men I spoke with were involved or knew other men involved in power plays with the women they were with and weren't sure how to proceed in the dating world, particularly online. Fraternity guys were more successful with women but even they had issues with the women they were dating.

In the following interviews I personally conducted with men, they described to me how these power plays by women and society that Gaines explores in his book apply in the world of dating, relationships, and beyond. They talked about their relationships with their fathers or lack thereof, the structural forces at work against them, and about the culture that views their masculinity as less than desirable, if not downright toxic. They also talked about a lack of purpose and the difficulty in not being needed or allowed to be themselves. In sum, they described all of the issues that the authors of the books I mentioned above, but their struggles in life were a combination of these factors rather than just one factor, as their interviews will demonstrate. Life is complex. The world has changed and often, not for the better, for either sex. Most of the men I talked to have overcome these obstacles but they are aware that their male sex makes life harder in many ways that few people understand.

The interviews with all the men have been edited for clarity and names and minor details have been changed to protect their identities. However, the substance and content remain true to their voices. I spoke to a diverse group of men of different ages, races and backgrounds, but what stands out is the common ground they all share when it comes to being men in a society that puts the needs and rights of women first and those of men last. The men were, for the most part, happy to talk and glad that someone wanted to listen to them. So seldom do men speak openly to a woman about what they *really* feel or think that some looked unsure about how to proceed while others looked relieved to have their say.

The young men speak first. Because they bear the brunt of much of the social change these days, I have two sections on young men—one on regular guys who shared thoughts on their lives and dating, and more specifically fraternity men who had more to say about college and women and being a young man today. Many young men are wise beyond their years and it is time that we listen to what *they* say instead of trying to speak for them and getting it wrong most of the time. Let's turn to what they think about dating, relationships, and their place in society.

CHAPTER TWO

Young Men Speak Out

*"If we want answers, we won't find them in the metrics,
but in the minds of the young men themselves."*

*Richard V. Reeves, author of Of Boys and Men:
Why the Modern Male Is Struggling, Why It
Matters, and What to Do About It*[54]

"I have a hard and fast rule, I don't kiss a girl at a party."

"I was on the baseball team and was told that we couldn't have a male locker room built because of Title IX. We were changing in a place that looked like a barn. We even got our own donors to give money and we never worked for anything harder in our lives."

"Colleges are skewed towards women."

---

[54] Richard V. Reeves, *Of Boys and Men: Why the Modern Male is Struggling, Why It Matters, and What to Do About It* (Brookings Institution Press, Washington DC, 2022), 74.

These are just some of the quotes I got from young men who realized early that the cards were stacked against them at colleges and other institutions that resent male success. Young men that I interviewed ten years ago when I wrote *Men on Strike* were more in the dark about the forces against them but today's young men are generally more savvy and aware of the problem. That is progress, though what to do about it is still an issue.

So what do younger men today in their twenties and early thirties think about being male in our society? What are the problems and concerns they have and how do they process the female-centered world they live in? The main themes I found with the men I interviewed were family issues, school, and occupational concerns, but mostly they were concerned about relationships with women. I started my search with a young man who is an athletic trainer, (let's call him Taylor)[55] who will be going to a doctoral program in physical therapy in the fall. He wants to work with kids, mainly boys in sports because there are so few male role models.

I told him I was writing a book about men's issues and asked him what the most important concern was of being a man in today's culture. "I think it's vulnerability," he stated.

"Huh, why is that?" I asked.

"Other men don't want you to be vulnerable, they are always competing and see you as a competitor. If you show feelings, you are seen as less than a man, they have one up on you. "

"What about women? How are they if you speak up and act vulnerable?" I asked.

---

[55] I have changed most names of interviewees to protect men's privacy, even if they said they didn't care. That said, some still insisted their names be used and I honored their wishes.

"Oh, they don't like it either. They feel you are not a man and might not be there for them as a guy." So neither sex likes a man to speak up or feel anything.

What this man is picking up on is our societal norm for men to keep their mouths shut and not whine, lest they be viewed as a burden rather than a helper and protector. Yet the female-centric society tells them to be vulnerable and to quit with the "toxic masculinity." This discrepancy between what men are told is "healthy and good" in modern men, and what the actual people in his life want and will put up with is confusing at best, and at worst, wreaks havoc with his inner life. This discrepancy theme was prevalent throughout my interviews—men are told to behave one way and if they do they are chastised or punished. And if they don't? They are chastised or punished. This next interviewee points out the hypocrisy of this damned if you do and damned if you don't behavior.

Next up is Keith, who is twenty-one and applying to grad schools. When I told him about my work, he smiled and said, "thanks for being on our team." I laughed and asked him what he thought of women his own age. He just graduated from undergrad and said that he enjoyed going to Jewish frat parties but he has a hard and fast rule, "I don't kiss a girl at a party. You don't know what will happen. There was a frat here at our school that was almost shut down because a girl got sick and drunk. This girl was drinking and went in the bathroom and took some kind of prescribed medicine but how can you know what she is doing? All the frats guys can't monitor all the women that come in here and it's not fair that we are expected to look after everyone that comes in who makes their own decisions. The frat got in trouble even though it wasn't their fault."

Keith has figured out early on that he and his male cohorts are held responsible for women's behavior (note the paternalistic expectations that guys are expected to monitor a girl's decisions). His way of dealing with it is to restrict his own behavior. Just don't get involved or touch a woman at a party. Not bad practical advice but grave responsibility for all men of college age who have enough trouble monitoring themselves. If a guy tells a woman what to do, he is sexist and has "toxic masculinity," but if he fails to supervise and protect her, he is responsible. No wonder most young guys are skittish about getting involved with women, especially at colleges.

And the statistics confirm that this avoidance is necessary. Title IX charges (sex discrimination complaints and sexual harassment) have skyrocketed in recent years. "The U.S. Department of Education's Office for Civil Rights received 18,804 complaints in fiscal year 2022—the most in its history and 12% higher than the previous record high of 16,720 complaints in 2016."[56] (It does turn out that one person made 7,339 of these allegations but this only shows how easy it is to file a charge against someone.) How many of these allegations are true? No one really knows, but one thing is for sure—men are the main targets of these complaints, and the younger guys like Keith know it. So if a young guy doesn't feel safe meeting a woman at college, there is always social media. But that comes with costs too.

Sometimes social media or even friends can help guys get out of the toxic college atmosphere and give them hope that a decent woman will come along. Will this work? It's not clear.

---

[56] Naaz Modan, "Office for Civil Rights fielded more Title IX complaints than any other kind in fiscal 2022," *Higher Ed Dive*, May 1, 2023. https://www.highereddive.com/news/OCR-title-ix-complaints-top-others-2022/649116/

The young men I interviewed had mixed feelings about using the dating apps. And as mentioned in the last chapter, the power plays that women use to show the upper hand are evident in both the dating apps and in the relationships the men later become involved in.

Blake

"I just don't think girls respect guys anymore."

My next interviewee, Blake, twenty-seven years old, discussed at length his experiences with dating apps like Tinder and social media as he chowed down on a sandwich (it looked amazing), and talked about life and living as a twenty-something in today's female-centered world. Blake describes himself as a solid eight-and-a-half, and has a lot to offer. He is tall and is an ex-ball player. One would think that this would make him super desirable as a potential date, but problems are prevalent even for men who are attractive and want a relationship.

"I get on the dating apps and it seems like even if you get a date, something always comes up with the girl. I get a message saying that they have some situation with their family or their dog. Funny how it always happens three hours before our date. In my mind, something better came along for her, some other guy on the app she found more interesting. I would say this happens about one out of every ten dates. The girls do it more often than guys, especially the more attractive girls because they get more offers."

"What are women that you meet on the apps like?" I asked.

"The girls vary in their attractiveness, but the ones that are sevens and above rarely even answer. They forget they are even on them sometimes. I will say hello and then after two sentences, you never hear from them again. It is very hard to meet people on these apps. I did go out on about five dates. One of them worked out for me. We still keep in touch."

"What was your worst date?"

"The worst date I had was horrible. We had a nice dinner—that was my first mistake. I shouldn't have taken her for an expensive dinner, it should have been a cup of coffee. But we hit it off. We hung out again after the first date. The second time we went out—we went downtown. We went in a bar and I went to the bathroom for a second and I came back out and looked for her for ten minutes. I texted her and was like, 'where did you go?' She said, 'I left, I was tired.' She was with a friend and she ghosted me. I would have respected her a lot more if she had just said she wanted to leave and I would have said, 'ok, you can leave. That's fine.' I just don't think girls respect guys anymore. I would rather someone on an app just say 'I am not interested' than just leave you wondering.

"I think it is the phones that are technically advanced that allow for this lack of respect today, with the apps and social media. When I was younger, it didn't happen as much. I think now that girls are more confident in their self-being. They just think, 'I don't need a man and why should I give him the time of day?' And they just ghost a guy. I have even seen video podcasts where girls just say, 'yeah I ghosted him.' This one girl, on her face, she seemed just super happy that she did it, that she ghosted some guy. It was rewarding to her. I think it felt empowering to her. Maybe like 'she got him.'"

Empowered or Mentally Unhealthy?

I noted that what men like Blake often call confidence or empowerment in a woman is actually more like revenge or manipulation. Men are indoctrinated early to use pro-female words like confidence or empowerment when a woman is just displaying bad behavior. Ghosting a guy is not empowerment or indicative of high self-worth. It is the result of someone who is entitled, unaware of the feelings of others, or worse, is aware and intentionally hurts people to make themselves feel better. Treating someone like garbage does not equal self-worth. In fact, it probably means they have low self-regard. As we see later, this low self-regard makes women more likely to externalize blame and treat men poorly.

If women, especially the younger ones these men are dating, really are so "empowered," then why do they self-describe as mentally unhealthy? Check out the graph in Figure 1 below that shows that over 50 percent of young women who are liberal say that they have been diagnosed with a mental health condition:

Pew (2020): "Has a doctor or healthcare provider EVER told you that you have a mental health condition?" % saying yes:

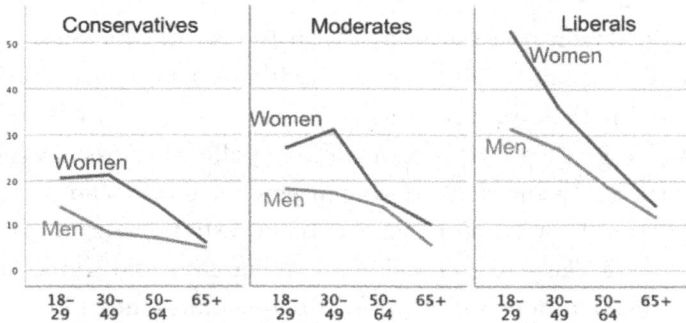

Figure 1. Data from Pew Research, American Trends Panel Wave 64. The survey was fielded March 19–24, 2020. Graphed by Jon Haidt.[57]

And it is not just the liberal women, it is also moderate and to a much lesser extent conservative women who answered "yes" to the question, "Has a doctor or healthcare provider EVER told you that you have a mental health condition?" Why is the mental health of women, especially liberal ones sinking so fast?

According to Jonathan Haidt, a prominent psychologist and author, it is largely because of the use of smart phones starting in 2012 and social media. Apparently liberal teen girls are using social media five or more hours a day (31 percent) and have less time for friends or social engagements "in real life." But even conservative girls are using it 22 percent. "[P]art of the story may be that social media took over the lives of liberal

<hr />

[57] Jon Haidt, "Why the Mental Health of Liberal Girls Sank First and Fastest," *After Babel,* March 9, 2023. https://www.afterbabel.com/p/mental-health-liberal-girls. *Data from* graph by John Haidt, "*American Trends Panel Wave 64, Pew Research, March 19–24, 2020.* https://www.pewresearch.org/social-trends/dataset/covid-19-late-march-2020/

girls more than any other group, and it is now clear that heavy use of social media damages mental health, especially during early puberty."[58]

But Haidt goes on to say that it is not just time on media that causes liberal girls mental health to sink, it is also the messaging that liberal girls get.[59] Younger women have become more progressive and more involved in political activism, which in turn has changed these women psychologically and not for the better. They are more likely to blame external sources (men) and more likely to feel bad about themselves and think they can't do anything right. And with good reason—they are taught to be victims and see the patriarchy as the enemy.

This means that men like Blake are smart to look for moderate, or conservative women on the dating apps. They are more likely to like men and less likely to blame them for their problems. Interestingly, young guys today are turning more to the right and this is why so many academics, the media and politicians are now starting to become more concerned about men.

But their concern hardly has to do with compassion. They just fear that men will get in the way of their power by voting against Democrats. Despite this, or maybe because of it, academics and the media can't help denigrating men and this disrespect and downright hostility sends a message to women and the general society that men do not deserve respect; and this disrespect plays its way into relationships, particularly in the often objectifying world of online dating, just as Blake noted.

---

[58] Haidt, "Why the Mental Health of Liberal Girls Sank First and Fastest."
[59] Ibid.

Preston

"I think guys feel uncomfortable, particularly in the home."

One of the first things I asked Preston, a thirty-one-year-old man who works at a car dealership in business development, was about how he felt at school when he was a kid. He is a nice-looking guy who seemed friendly and good-natured now, but I knew from speaking with a family member that school had been hard for him. He had moved to a new area with his older sister and parents when he was young. His sister loved going to a new school and told me she met her first day with, "Hello world, I'm Tessa!" In contrast, Preston felt upset and anxious around new students and started to become depressed. Why am I telling you this? Because guys moving to new areas, even better ones, when they are young can cause emotional reactions similar to PTSD in soldiers[60] and no one really acknowledges this or cares. The idea of moving and the fear boys have of making new friends and dealing with a new environment can carry forward into later life and cause anxiety and a lack of confidence, even with dating and later relationships. I will be discussing this theme of moving throughout the book. Next, I asked Preston about online dating.

Many of the young men I spoke with mentioned social media dating sites as a necessary evil when it comes to meeting someone special. They were often post college and didn't love the bar scene, which makes online dating one of the few options. Preston reported that he and another guy at work

---

[60] Andrew M. Seaman, "Moving out of poverty linked to kids' mental health," *Reuters*, March 4, 2014. https://www.reuters.com/article/business/healthcare-pharmaceuticals/moving-out-of-poverty-linked-to-kids-mental-health-idUSBREA2324K/

got on social media to try and find dates and had some mixed results. Preston didn't like the objectifying nature of the apps which made dating seem less human. "If you are twenty-one to twenty-five, you can go to a bar but it is not my scene. How do you meet someone in your thirties now? Especially since COVID, you are not sitting across from someone where you just meet and talk and stuff, you are looking at five pictures online at a time.

"I tried Tinder, Bumble and I want to try Hinge. I met this one girl on Tinder. But I swiped through a lot of women to find her. It gets to the point where you just sit there for hours and swipe. I finally just put my phone down and say to myself, 'this is such a waste of time.'

"Most of the women seem very unprofessional."

"What do you mean?" I asked.

"The girls seem mostly interested in hook-ups or they want someone to do something with. I feel that I am professional and hardworking but it's hard to meet someone like that on an app. There seemed to be few people interested in long-term relationships. I was so against apps for a long time but it got to the point where I thought 'how was I going to meet someone?' It is so rare to find someone pretty with a good job. I like to have in-depth conversations and talk deeply about things, and it is a very shallow environment."

As for prior relationships, Preston says he had a girlfriend in college and later "met a woman when I was twenty-eight at a party, and we dated but she had two kids, two and six. We faded out because I wasn't as settled down as she was. This past Christmas I dated a woman from Tinder I met for three months, but that fizzled out."

Preston feels that for now, there is much to single life that he enjoys and he likes "being free....I think guys are less interested in getting married now, or maybe society is less interested in marriage. I talk to younger guys and now nobody thinks about getting married until their thirties anymore. Growing up in my culture [in Tennessee], you got married at twenty-five and had kids and that was it. I feel bad about myself because here I am at thirty-one and all my friends are married and have kids. I want that at some point.... Most of the women my age are divorced, or divorced and have a couple of kids. It is rare to meet women who have not been married. That is probably more common in Tennessee rather than in a big city."

"Women don't expect as much these days. Women want to be professional and don't just want a provider."

"Where does that leave guys?" I asked.

"I think it leaves them in an awkward position. I have a friend who is a woman in her forties who is going to get a divorce and she tells her husband, 'I don't need you.' She is a strong woman."

"How would you feel if a woman told you that?" I asked.

"That would make me feel terrible. She threatens divorce and says she has a good job when he says something to her. If you are the provider, you would feel more stability. If you both have good jobs, it is easier for the women to move on."

Men Feel Uncomfortable

I asked Preston about how men feel about their place in the home to which he replied, "I think guys feel uncomfortable." As an example, he stated, "my friend told me that last night he went to eat some Alfredo out of the fridge, and his girlfriend wanted to take it to lunch tomorrow, and he put it back and then she started bawling and crying saying that she had been mean and she wanted him to hold her while she was sobbing. When I heard that, part of me thought I really enjoy being single. The food was both of theirs and after he put it back and she realized that he felt controlled, she felt bad and started crying. Maybe this makes her feel more comfortable but there is just this emotion between the two people can fluctuate so much."

"Do men and women have different emotional reactions?" I asked.

"Yes, I think so, he said. "It can vary of course, but generically I think men are not quite as comfortable showing emotion as women. If men show an emotion, it may be anger. They don't feel as comfortable crying or getting upset about something. Guys don't cry, they get angry."

"But what would happen if guys starting crying to their girlfriends?" I asked.

Preston stated that he thought guys *should* be able to cry.

"But what would happen if they did?"

"I think some women would think the man was not as strong or she may feel differently about that person showing an emotion and think 'you are not supposed to do that, you're a guy. You're supposed to be strong.' But there are some women who don't feel that way. But I do think men hold in their emotions. My friends wouldn't feel super comfortable crying in front of their girlfriends. Women have a wider range of emotions they can express. It is not as taboo for a woman to show more emotion. Both sexes feel this way about men. Men want to seem that they can provide, or if the woman is upset, they can be strong but inside they may feel differently."

Men are told repeatedly that they need to be in touch with their emotions and show how they feel, particularly with a woman. But the young men in my interviews knew instinctively that opening up to a woman was the wrong move, one that would show them to be weak and unable to provide and in turn, to be viewed as a poor partner. Women and the media can go on all they want that men are closed off cavemen who just can't deal with a strong woman but the truth is, polls show that men and women alike believe the man should be a provider and being a provider means being strong for a woman.

Notwithstanding the march of feminism, stats show this to be the prevailing view today: "Roughly seven-in-ten adults (71%) say it is very important for a man to be able to support a family financially to be a good husband or partner. By comparison, 32% say it's very important for a woman to do the same to be a good wife or partner, according to a new Pew Research Center survey."[61] Some women can say they don't mind being a provider, but in the end, like Preston's friend who is getting divorced, women often throw their high earnings in the face of men to essentially say, "I don't need you. I need a man like a fish needs a bicycle."

Psychological Warfare

In the first chapter, I mentioned Richard Reeves, who called this lack of need for men "cultural redundancy" and blamed it on structural changes in our society. What he doesn't point out, but that Preston's interview illustrates, is that women are using the fact that they have jobs and make money as psychological warfare against the men that they are supposed to love.

---

[61] Kim Parker and Renee Stepler, "Americans see men as the financial providers, even as women's contributions grow," Pew Research Center, September 20, 2017. https://www.pewresearch.org/short-reads/2017/09/20/americans-see-men-as-the-financial-providers-even-as-womens-contributions-grow/

This is at the crux of the malaise that many men feel. They are being psychologically belittled by women and by the society that encourages this behavior and no one talks about it. If a man speaks up, he finds himself ridiculed further or tagged as a misogynist. Or worse, he is told he is expendable and no longer needed by a woman who once professed to love him. It's a surprise that even more aren't MGTOW ("men going their own way" and choosing to find happy lives without a woman).

On the other hand, some men *want* to be with a woman but are withdrawing into video games or other pursuits to avoid the rejection they fear they will face if they ask a woman out. This seemed to be the case with Hudson, a kind twenty-seven-year-old who works as a perfusionist (he operates the heart/lung machine) at a hospital and hasn't had a girlfriend since college.

Hudson

"The cool thing to be is an atheist. As a religious person, I feel I can't speak up sometimes."

"I'm also short. Girls are looking for taller guys."

Hudson stopped by my office one day after work for his interview and seemed both shy and reserved. He has dark hair and looked to be around five foot eight or so and I noticed that he seemed a bit reluctant at times to talk, which made it difficult to access what he really thought about today's dating and social scene. That said, he was very thoughtful and reflected on his answers about women, dating and his life in general. As I often do with these interviews, I asked him what he thought a good men's center would be like and he said it would "probably center around sports and activities. I think of it kind of like the

YMCA where men have activities and I guess this would get them to talk more." Hudson seemed to like camaraderie with men, and he and his friends generally bond over sports or exercise and he feels he can talk to them if he has an issue. Speaking with women in today's awkward and superficial dating market is another matter.

Hudson went to a private Catholic school though he is not Catholic, and grew up as a Christian. He stated that it is "not popular to be religious and the cool thing to be is an atheist." He is looking for "a conservative Christian woman with strong values who likes sports and children," which has been hard for him to find. When he was younger, he dated a girl in high school but they broke up when they went to undergrad as she moved. He went to college at a large public Southern school and met a woman there who was also Christian and they dated for about six months. "We broke up because we weren't compatible." "In what way?" I asked. "We did not enjoy the same things. She liked artsy things and I am more logical. I like to talk about science and politics and things like that. Most girls like Netflix shows and can't have a conversation about current and world events. Some girls seem to care more about a show than what is happening in the world."

He feels that his ideal mate is elusive, as he is no longer in school, works mainly with men, and has nowhere to turn except the dating apps.

"Have you tried online dating?" I asked.

"Not really, I think the girls are more superficial and have certain requirements."

"Like what?"

"Well, they want a guy with a high paying job who is six feet and muscular."

"Does that make it harder for you?"

"I think so, I am also introverted. And I want someone committed to their relationships and someone who is loyal. I think it is hard in today's world to find that, probably because the country is not as religious as it used to be. It's more acceptable to hook up with different people all the time."

Hudson feels that social media plays a part in women being more picky as they have more options to pick and choose than men. "They are also more independent now which puts them in the position when they do want to get married to be choosier since they might be fine alone. They expect more."

"Does this make it harder for regular guys to find women to marry?"

"Yes," he stated. "It does. Men feel that it is tougher than it was, for sure."

"Are the women looking for something you are not?" I asked.

"Yes, I feel, I don't know the specific word here, maybe I feel not great?" At this point in the interview, Hudson tried not to choke up. "I would say I feel worried. Worried that I will not match up to what women are expecting. Worried that I will never find someone. I am afraid I will not measure up."

Dating While Short

There is much truth to what Hudson says—it is harder for men who are shorter than six feet to find women, but of course it is not impossible. This internal monologue that Hudson repeats to himself—that he is not getting dates because he is under six feet and is not good enough—is common for many men in the dating world now, and many, like Hudson have bailed out of the game in order to avoid rejection. Hudson is reluctant to go out and actually talk with and interact with women and this fear of rejection is keeping him home playing video games in his room. A friend of his confirmed this, stating that Hudson often mentioned being short when they would be at a gym or restaurant where women were present, or he would avoid going out at all for fear of women rejecting him for being short. He shrugged off these feelings when I asked him about them. However, when I asked him what bothered him most about not finding a woman, he softly stated, "I would be all alone."

Sadly, Hudson is onto something. Women in today's modern society prefer tall men, as evidenced by the following graph from the American Perspectives Survey[62] that shows 56 percent of women surveyed would not want a man who is much shorter.

Height Matters More To Women Than It Does To Men

Percentage of Americans who said they would be *less* likely to date someone who is . . .

	Much Shorter	Much Taller
Men	11	32
Women	56	8

Survey Center on American Life

Note: Survey of US adults (N = 5,055).
Source: American Perspectives Survey, January 2023.

Following up on Hudson's feeling that being short is a deal killer when it comes to getting a date, I set out to find another man who was under six feet to see if he had a similar experience. My next interviewee, Jake, is around five feet nine, and he not only agreed that being short made things more difficult but had a lot of firsthand experience with the dating apps with which to

---

[62] Daniel A. Cox, "From Swiping to Sexting: The Enduring Gender Divide in American Dating and Relationships," *American Perspectives Survey*, February 9, 2023. https://www.americansurveycenter.org/research/from-swiping-to-sexting-the-enduring-gender-divide-in-american-dating-and-relationships/#_edn8. See also: Rob Henderson, "Swiping and Dating Preferences," *Rob Henderson's Newsletter*, July 23, 2023. https://www.robkhenderson.com/p/swiping-and-dating-preferences

draw his conclusions. But unlike Hudson, he understood how to make up for what he lacked in stature by developing other qualities that women on the dating apps were looking for. He is also more outgoing, which helps. He explained to me the limitations of being under six feet as a guy and went more in depth into why and how the dating apps take the humanity out of human relationships. In addition, most of the apps have led to women demanding ever increasing requirements for men if they want to get a date or even talk to them. The majority of men never make the cut. It's common for women to ask about wanting a man with "the three sixes"—a six figure income, at least six feet tall, and with at least a six-inch penis. That's not most men, leaving women feeling deprived and men feeling devalued.

Jake

"Per a study, only 1.5 out of 100 males in the US are making more than 70K annually, are 5 feet 10 inch or taller, have hair and are not obese."[63]

Jake is a thirty-four-year-old entrepreneur in Florida who came ready with a set with notes and a keen interest in the world of online dating. He even sent me links to online Twitter (now X) mentions of how hard it is for a normal man to get a date as most women's expectations are way out of line with reality, as evidenced by the quote above stating that only 1.5 percent of men meet the criteria of most women on internet dating boards.

[63] Tic toc (@TicTocTick), "Per a study," X, October 31, 2023. https://twitter.com/TicTocTick/status/1719501872892191194

Jake was a fun interview. He met me at a Starbucks and asked if he could buy me a coffee. "No thanks," I said, "I should be buying one for you, since you agreed to do this interview to help me with my book." Like many guys, he would not hear of a woman paying for her own food or drinks, even if it was a psychologist picking his brain for clues into the male mind. I was kind of amazed at the generosity and polite nature of most of the men I interviewed and Jake was no exception.

Now There Are Two Hunters

When I told Jake I was writing a book about the male mind and men's thoughts and feelings about modern society, he stated, "the brain of a man is different. It's amazing that men and women can even coexist. They want different things. Take relationships. Women want a very fairy-tale marriage or relationship where men are pretty simple. We just want support for the things we lack as a man. A man can bring things to the table that a woman can't and vice versa. It's simple stuff like a clean home or a cooked meal. I would want my woman to have more time, I want to be the main provider. Going back to hunting and gathering, I think the man provides and the woman is the main supporter at the house.

"With the new modern day women and their lifestyle, the dynamics have changed. Women's roles have changed; they are working harder. Now you are both hunting at the same time. Now there are two hunters on the scene. Things are lacking for a man, a man is just looking for support. I believe that women are the nurturers for children. I think the man should go out and work. My mom had to raise three of us alone and I think I watched her struggle. My mom worked during the night and my dad during the day and they got divorced. She was in multiple marriages but for the most part she was a solo parent. But my dad had shared parenting after he moved back to Florida from Minnesota." Jake did mention that there were many years that he did not see his father much.

Jake dated a woman while he was in college and she was older, like twenty-three when he was nineteen or twenty. When she graduated, they went their own way. "She expected a lot too quick, marriage, kids. She was on the fast track and I was trying to finish school. Post college, I dated a college student for two years, but I was focused on my business, which was taking off, so we eventually broke up. I wanted to be successful and only saw her one or two days a week and she eventually left for someone who could give her more time."

Jake has his own boat and car rental business and does very well. He tried working an entry job in the corporate world for six months but didn't like it and has spent the past ten years or more as an entrepreneur. He spent a good deal of our interview explaining how his business works and the risks he took to get where he is today. "Business was great, the money was great, but I'm not great." He feels that he is now ready for a serious relationship but getting there has been a struggle.

Economics Makes Relationships Harder

I asked Jake why so many people today have trouble finding a relationship and he replied "relationships are harder in general now. I think the pressure comes in part from the high cost of living. Now, a man has to make at least $150,000 or more to pay for everything and everyone does have to work harder. The cost of a house is so much more than it used to be. It puts pressure on both sides to bring in that kind of income.

"I think women want a guy that makes a lot. Everyone wants a nice car, a nice house. Women are making more money now and they are bringing something to the table but they want the man to make more and it makes everything more competitive. It used to be that women had easier going jobs and now they have a lot more stress trying to be a CEO or some high job placement."

Online Dating Is Brutal

"Online dating is brutal," he remarked later in the interview. "How so?" I asked. "Well, it's the same problem that plagues all of society; a lack of humanity. People are losing empathy for one another, expecting flawless partners and relationships and thinking others are mere objects at their disposal. Some of the biggest reasons for the lack of humanity include technology being more advanced and dating has become more impersonal. People feel at risk putting their pictures up online where people they know could see it. While dating has always presented challenges; dating, love, and relationships seem even more complicated today with the apps."

The Dating Apps

"I moved out to Colorado when I was twenty-eight and started using Tinder, but it was mainly a hook-up scene. People are on there just for quick entertainment and quick pleasure. It was just swipe left or right on a picture and that was it.

"Then Bumble hit the scene and it was better. There were many pictures, you can get more filters for the person you are looking for, even down to if they want kids or what kinds of political beliefs they have. It is different now with politics, you used to be able to have a civil conversation over coffee and I did have a few dates with women that were liberal. Today, you would have no chance to have a civil conversation. I am Republican and like to talk about issues but liberals today stand on a fine line. I could not date a liberal, it is crazy to say that. But there would be a topic that I could cope with but they couldn't. There would be communication problems.

"With Bumble, the filters mean that you can choose what you want. Height, kids, not kids, it puts this unrealistic perfect image in your mind and it is hard to find someone who checks all the boxes. There is always something imperfect with any relationship. You put yourself in a situation where only a few people on the app meet the requirements and you have to compromise to make a relationship work.

"For an attractive woman, they are getting thousands and thousands of interested men so their options are endless. A man doesn't have that. Because of the endless options, a man really has to stand out. The women can have really high criteria as a result. I believe women want money, success, status. Women want to be seen in pictures like on Instagram on a trip and in a nice car; a woman is not going to date a broke dude. She is going to be harsh. Men may not get many matches at all. On Bumble, it is up to the woman to match up if the guy swipes right, the guy can't message a woman but if she has thousands of matches, she may not even see his profile. The woman is in full control on Bumble which gives her power—which is great—but she may only pick a few guys that she matched with.

"On Hinge, it is different, the problem is the man has to have a striking pick up line to get a woman. They really have to stand out, maybe with humor, or a man can buy what is called Roses on Hinge or a SuperSwipe on Bumble that is sent to the woman to let her know he is very interested. The man is pumping in money to stand out. These apps are making millions of dollars off desperate men wanting a date on a Friday night." That said, it seemed like Jake was one of the men spending money to stand out and get dates, perhaps to make up for what he thought was his shortcoming—being less than six feet. It is possible that his lack of confidence had to do with reality with the women in Tampa, Florida, and what they expected. Or it could be his lack of confidence about other aspects of his life.

Attention Is a Drug for Many Women

Jake did feel that women used the internet for ulterior motives other than dating. He continued, "women are on the apps to get attention—maybe to get followers for Only Fans or Instagram. Girls are often not even looking for relationships. A girl with 50,000 followers can get brand deals or something. Women like attention; they want to be seen, to be looked at. They thrive on attention. A girl with full makeup and all dressed up gets looked at, the girl in the sweatshirt and no makeup doesn't get looked at. Attention is a drug for many women. The majority of women are like this. It is a need for status.

"And men seek out all that, the status, the pretty woman. A man has to be happy with who he looks at. For me in my life, I want that support, someone who will support me but at the same time, I am used to a certain level of good looks."

Height Requirements

"I am five foot nine, shorter to normal I guess, but I notice most women's profiles say six feet or over." "How do you cope with that?" I asked. Jake looked thoughtful and stated, "In my opinion, I would not want to date a woman taller than me. A man wants to be a strong guy, but I am talking about a girl six foot two. If she is five foot four, why do you need a guy over six feet? I think women love the masculine energy of taller men and maybe that correlates with wanting a taller, stronger man. They do not want a small dude that is not built. For guys who are shorter than that, what do we do? There will be a girl out there for you. It's depressing though, because you do not fit the bill of what these girls are into or want. If you are five feet eleven or less, you are just filtered out. The majority of women filter out for height. The filter opens the door up to this finite perfect person that women think they can get."

"Did you ever get any dates with all the restrictions?" I asked. "Yes, I got about ten dates over time. I went to my dates in public. Many of the dates want to drink, like cocktails to break the ice. But at the end of the day, my being five foot nine, the women knew there was someone better out there for them. They could get on the app and have endless options.

"The women are unrealistic, they are more unrealistic than men. Women can improve themselves much more than men with all the plastic surgery, and liposuction is out there whereas men are not going to do this. So technically, a woman who is a four in looks could get up to an eight or a ten. Men are stuck with what we have. As a man, we do none of this. If we are a six, we're a six. A woman can go up. There is Botox on every street corner. Women are more resigned to do all of these things if they want to get dates."

Nines or Tens Are Undatable

"What about dating such attractive women?" I asked. Jake answered, "Maybe it is not great to have the nines and tens because they get so much attention and may look beautiful, but you will deal with a lot more in a relationship. You go out and they stick out and are wanted. The nines and tens don't know how to date, they are not long-term material because they believe there is more out there for them, and they can leave and get someone else. She knows it will be so easy to get another date or match. It is mostly when people are younger that they do this. As they get older, they become more mature. And the dynamic changes. My new girlfriend is beautiful but she is older and more mature."

So Jake's story initially had a happy ending. He was in a good relationship with a woman who, when someone said "your guy is short," replied, "So what? I'm short too." Jake had the confidence to hang in there and find a wonderful partner for a while. Sadly, things did not work out with the relationship but it did last a year, which in these days of revolving relationships is no small feat.

Young guys deserve another chapter as they are on the forefront of the gender wars in today's polarized world. The next chapter will focus on young men's views at a large Southern university and what they have to say about being male at a school that is a majority women (around 54 percent female, 46 percent male). These are actually good odds, given that many universities such as the University of Vermont are roughly 36 percent male, 64 percent female.[64] I took my small tape recorder, a notepad and a positive attitude and headed over to meet a group of frat guys who were kind enough to share their opinions with me after I met one of the fraternity brothers who asked his housemates to participate.

---

[64] "University of Vermont Student Life," *U.S. News & World Report.* https://www.usnews.com/best-colleges/university-of-vermont-3696/student-life

CHAPTER THREE

Frat Guys Speak Out

"**D**ouchebags, Alcoholics, F**k Boys."

"A bunch of shirtless guys who only care about partying and being scummy to women, there is a negative connotation to the term fraternity."

"A sexually-focused male."

These are just some of the responses I got when I asked the group of fraternity guys what stereotypes people think of when they hear the word fraternity. I was sitting with a group of seniors at a large SEC university in their house off campus. There were six or seven guys wandering in and out who stopped by to be interviewed and a core group who sat with me on the couch and let me pick their brains about what it is like to be a young fraternity guy on campus. All the men were twenty-one or twenty-two and graduating soon with degrees ranging from logistics, finance, and business to kinesiology. All of the guys are success stories for making it through the university system, managing dating relationships and having great friendships among themselves. Their stories should serve as examples to high school or younger guys who want to learn to navigate through the university system successfully.

Their house dog, a "mutt" named Theo found on Craigslist came by happily to see what all the excitement was about, and spent his time running from one person to the next. He was eventually scooped up by one of the guys, Sam, who arrived later with the dog lovingly wrapped in a towel after his bath. Theo's life looked pretty good.

Southern Versus Northern Frat Guys

"Why do you think people have such a negative image of fraternities?" I asked once I had petted the dog. A tall good-looking guy, Ben, a twenty-one-year-old senior in business spoke up that he felt that it was the northern guys that came down to join a fraternity that were the worst.

"I think they watch *Jersey Shore* and think that is what fraternities are about," Ben said. "The southern men are more traditional, for the most part, with the traditional being focused on friendship, service and being a gentleman. The northern guys love to party and use women. These men are northern conservatives. I am somewhat conservative too, but the way we go about things is wildly different. The northern guys are trying to escape the more Democratic North, they use being conservative as an out to get out of the structure that they had up there."

"You are definitely an outlier if you are a liberal in a fraternity. Conservatives are more the norm," Max added. "But the northern guys who say they are conservative come down here and get a little crazy."

"Why is that? I asked.

Daniel, a twenty-one-year-old working in supply chain management chimed in, "I think the North is so Catholic-centralized and drinking or anything is more frowned upon. But here when we were growing up, drinking was seen as more of a part of living. I would drink wine when I was around thirteen with my parents. We would do more grown-up things but under supervision."

Max added that he would hide his drinking from the family but one day he opened up and talked to his dad and told him that he drank heavily with his friends. "After that, my life was a lot easier and I eased up on drinking." Just the act of telling his dad helped Max to realize that he did not need to drink so much. Max continued, "Northern guys will do a lot of destructive things to themselves like turning to drugs. In the past three years, our school has let in a lot more out of state students and it has changed the dynamic."

Ben interjected with, "Northern guys were used to a different family structure that is more permissive than traditional southern families. They come down here from Delaware, New York, Maryland, Chicago and northern Virginia, that kind of area. They are more bad apples, more prone to be using hard core drugs than the southern guys. Southern guys stick to drinking and a little marijuana."

A few other guys chimed in with, "there are a few bad apples, stuff you see about frat guys on the news or any form of media or in movies—they are always portrayed as a negative thing. It is hard to explain the values of being in a fraternity."

"What are the values?" I asked. Ben answered, "every single Greek organization has their own set of staple values. Ours are friendship, knowledge, service, morality and excellence. We walk our pledges through these values and talk about how to build each other up."

Male Friendships

"Are these male friendships important for men?" I queried.

"Yes, I believe so, said Ben. "I think men and women are so different. It is hard to pinpoint but I think your male friends will be more honest with you."

Another member of the group, Max, a twenty-one-year-old majoring in sports medicine, answered that male friends are extremely honest and will call you out when you are being a jerk or will point out when your behavior is unacceptable.

"Like a moral compass?" I asked.

Max replied, "If someone is off, we try to draw them back. If someone is in a bad mood in the house and says something negative, I will give it right back to you if you're a guy. But with my girlfriend, I handle it totally differently. I would never do that. I would de-escalate."

Other men agreed that it would be best with their girlfriend to tone it down. Another member of the group, Daniel, the supply chain major, chimed in, "A bunch of girls getting up in the morning is not going to treat each other like that. They are going to go talk to their other friends, as far as we know." Daniel thoughtfully stated, "girls are more empathetic."

It struck me that what they are saying is that they are direct with their housemates whereas women would talk to each other about what their roommates had done that they did not like rather than speak directly to them. "Women are more empathetic to other people's feelings." Another guy chimed in, "Guys want to be talked to, girls want to be listened to. I think guys are just brutally honest."

"But isn't honesty a form of empathy?" I asked. "It can be," said Daniel, "but in some ways, it can also not be at all. Sometimes the honesty part skips empathy and goes towards something you didn't want to hear."

Girls Like to Rant

Max said that rather than complain, "girls like to rant. They like to tell you how they feel."

"Do you ever offer advice to a girl?" I asked.

"I do," Max answered, "but not every girl wants to hear that. They would rather be listened to."

Daniel, who has had a girlfriend for four years that he met in high school said that for him, it was different. Over the years, he has learned to just listen to what his girlfriend wants to say and only give advice if she asks for it. He added, "rant is a good word, I think because if you say a girl complains, it sounds like you don't care what they are saying. In reality, a rant is explaining how you feel about something."

Another guy, twenty-two-year-old Carter, who is in finance, spoke up to say that a rant for a girl could mean telling you that they are in the right, which they need for assurance.

"Do guys need that assurance that they are right?" I asked.

"I think it is a sense of pride for guys that they like to be right. But guys become angry if they are accused of being wrong," added another guy. "Guys will be upset for a few hours but would get over it."

"Would you ever tell your girlfriend she was wrong if you thought she was?" I asked Daniel, since he had a long-term girlfriend.

"Hmm, no because I feel like my job is to always be supportive." Max felt that his girlfriend was supportive and added that it is "a balance." Most of the guys seemed fairly sophisticated about their relationships; their maturity was inspiring as they seemed to really love women and understand them in a way that I wondered if their girlfriends reciprocated. The guys were open and seemed sincere about offering their feelings and opinions about their lives as friends. When one guy wanted to share more about his troubles as a kid, I felt like I was participating in a group therapy session instead of hanging out at a frat house.

Trouble with Dad

Ben opened up about his home life, stating that his dad was an alcoholic and drug user when he was young. "I was from Nashville. My dad was abusive to my mom and she had to get a restraining order."

"Did he hit you?" I asked.

"No, he hit my sisters. It was weird because he seemed to show favoritism to me, like 'this is my son, my prized possession.' During the two years after he left when I was ten or eleven, I tried to step up and care for my sisters and I leaned on my faith. That is where I became a believer. I remember vividly crying in my bathroom one night on my hands and knees and asking the Lord, 'Why would you do this to my mom and my family?'" Ben read me a Bible verse from Isaiah 41:10 that he carries in his wallet to remind him to persevere in hard times. This verse and his faith is what has kept him going:

So do not fear, for I am with you;
do not be dismayed, for I am your God.
I will strengthen you and help you;
I will uphold you with my righteous right hand.

Ben still has no real relationship with his biological dad. "I try to see him when I go home but there is no sign of any kind of progress. I think he has some mental problems. He denies everything, the addiction to alcohol or drugs. He denies he has problems with anger and said he never raised his voice. I have vivid memories of the complete opposite on an almost nightly basis." Ben's mother remarried when he was in seventh grade and Ben said, "My stepdad was very different. He is a very strong believer."

One of Ben's friends said that Ben had a long time relationship from high school with a girl who told him recently that they needed to break up because he would not be rich enough for her. Ben did not mention this but his friend felt that he still had feelings for her, despite her treating him poorly. Max spoke up to say that he also had a dad who had abused alcohol and drugs, and his parents divorced as a result. He reflected that his dad was afraid of failure and had turned to abusing substances to compensate. He was also aware that he did not play a part in his dad leaving the family. This knowledge seemed to be key in his becoming successful at college and at life. Often, when men feel they are to blame when their father leaves the house, they have less confidence and self-esteem. But when they can analyze the situation and realize they are not to blame, they seem to do well. This is why it is important to help dad-deprived boys understand that they are not responsible for dad leaving.

Wanting to know more about the dads the men discussed, I talked to a family member about Max's dad, and she remarked that David (Max's father) had moved around a lot as a kid while his parents were in the Air Force. He found it hard to make friends and settle into a new environment and felt that it affected him later in life, causing stress, anxiety, and resulting substance abuse. While other factors were probably at play, when boys move often, it can produce a PTSD effect that may lead to coping problems as an adult. If we become more aware that boys need additional help in adjusting to moves and new schools, it can go a long way in boys doing better in life.

College, Politics and Being a Guy in Class

Turning away from family matters and onto how their colleges were handling the politically charged atmosphere recently with the war in Israel and other political hot button topics, most of the guys agreed that there were few, but mostly peaceful protests at the SEC schools as opposed to the universities in other regions. "I think SEC schools in general have missed the rallies and protests that more northern schools have, or the protests will be smaller. Most of the pro-Palestinian protests were small here and pretty peaceful," Ben stated. "The worst protests usually are the anti- and proabortion groups who set up across from each other and get pretty rowdy. I think schools here in the South are a little better, especially ours, for having more peaceful protests."

I asked the group more specifically about being in class as conservative guys. Were there issues that they had, and if so, what were they? Did they feel they could speak up? The worst place to be as a conservative guy, according to the group, was English class. Ben added, "the professors there, the way they teach, they show their political liberal ideology up front. The last English class I was in the professor announced on the first day, 'first things first, let's all address our pronouns.' My teacher was a she/they. I feel like this is a liberal way of thinking."

"But did you feel you would get a bad grade if you did not go along with the pronoun announcement or any other liberal requests?" I asked.

"Yes, I did," Ben replied. "I felt like she would make it *seem* like she was asking for my honest opinion but..." At this point, the rest of the group chimed in with, "we've never tested the waters with this." Daniel continued, "We all just write our papers in a way that will get an A. We are taught to write to our readers, and I knew my teacher was my reader, and I knew she would like my paper if I wrote it a certain way. I would just attempt to make the paper be progressive sounding and always be a fence-sitter on political issues. Our teacher wanted us to participate in class and if I spoke, it was to give a viewpoint that she would appreciate more." Other guys added in that, if the conversation was non-political, they felt okay speaking up. But if it was political, "you don't want to cause an issue for yourself in the classroom."

Daniel said that he does not encounter too much political conversation because he is in supply chain management and it is not generally political.

"Do you like that it is not as political?" I asked.

"I do," he said. "I think men usually gravitate towards majors that men usually do." Most of the frat guys were in fields that were not as female dominated, like business or finance. I asked the guys if they would go into a field like nursing.

"My girlfriend is in nursing and I can guarantee that I would not do it," said Daniel. "The asks of the job are not for me. The medical field is kind of gross."

"What about you, Max?" I asked. "Could you go into a field like teaching or nursing?"

"I could be a history teacher, I guess. But I couldn't be a nurse. The pay is not great. I do think that nurses deserve more pay."

At this point, Daniel asked if I thought that, for women, pay didn't matter as much, and that maybe women cared more about the job and were willing to do it for less. We discussed this possibility for a while though I pointed out that as a woman, I cared very much about the pay but at the same time, saw my peers in psychology who were female were willing to work for less. "Would a scholarship for these fields like nursing make a difference to men?" I asked. "Maybe," they said, though most of them looked skeptical.

Core Values and Family

Daniel explained why men might have a hard time taking a job with lower pay such as nursing or social work. "I know that in the future, I will be taking care of not just myself but my future family. I think that is a core value of what being a man is—they are a provider. I know that I want to do something that is going to allow me to provide for my kids in the future. I want three or four kids." At this point I asked some of the other men how many kids they wanted. "Three or four" was the typical answer. "So the core value of a man is to provide?" I asked. "I want my wife to stay home unless she wants to work at something she has a passion for," said Max, "but don't waste your time working a nine to five if I can provide." The other men in the group nodded along with this notion—they felt that a husband should provide for the family and only if the woman feels like it, should she have to go out and work.

"Huh, well, what do you think of a society that sends a double message to men, that they are no longer supposed to provide or that the wife can, even though most women (and society) expect the man to do so in marriage?" I asked.

Daniel spoke up, "good for you if that is what you want to do, but I disregard this as I will try to provide as much as I possibly can for my family."

"Wouldn't it be hard to provide for your wife and kids?" I asked.

Ben spoke up. "You have to find a balance to where you can provide for them in a way—not just the home and food but psychological needs."

"What kind of psychological needs?" I asked. "The man should be the total foundation of the home," said Max. Some of the other guys said, "Well not the total foundation." Another man spoke up, "Women provide love."

"What if the woman is not that good at this?" I asked.

Ben replied, "You found the wrong partner then." Daniel added "I think that is something you find while dating in college. You are looking for more than a person to hang out with, you are looking for someone who is checking the boxes you are looking for."

"What qualities are you looking for in a wife?"

"Being able to provide for the family in a motherly way, in a way that a man like me can't provide, emotionally and

spiritually," said Daniel. "My girlfriend has all of these qualities." Both of Daniel's parents are together and he is the youngest of four children from Nashville. "All four of us are out of the
house and my parents are very happy together. I learned from
them what a family unit should look like, at least in my eyes."

"What about people who don't have that experience or see
what a happy family looks like?" I asked.

Daniel considered. "It does make it harder, but that is not
to say that other guys would not be able to have a good family.
I was fortunate. My dad taught us from a young age to respect
each other as a family and to respect other people."

"Do you think guys need a dad?"

"I do," said Daniel, "or at least a father figure in their
life." Some of his other roommates in the previous section had
mentioned not having a dad in the home or their parents were
divorced and Daniel was empathetic to their situation with this
statement, despite stating earlier that men were just direct or
blunt with each other. "Some people aren't able to have a dad
but having a father figure is part of maturing as a man. It is
learning what a man is supposed to be, how you are supposed
to act, or react to hardships." "Yeah," mumbled some of the
other guys in the group, including some who hadn't spoken
up as much.

Fear of Failure, Procrastination
Lead to Apathy, Self-Sabotage

"I think the danger of life for men is failure."

Twenty-one-year-old Max

Daniel continued with some philosophical advice he got from his dad. "We were just talking about hardships recently at my house. Sometimes bad things just happen, but you keep pushing through. I think of all the possibilities and everything negative that can go wrong. But I learned from my dad that you don't have to fix everything because things can just go wrong, and even if you make a mistake, you will be okay. It is too much overthinking that leads to problems, my dad said. And it was true. The more I worried over things, the more I would procrastinate."

"Do you think guys procrastinate due to fear of failure that they can't push through?" I asked.

"Yes, I do," said Daniel, and the other guys chimed in, "Some guys have this burden and it gets so pent up, they can't see their way through, it's overwhelming."

"What's the burden?" I asked Daniel.

"The burden is being a good man." Max acknowledged that his own father had felt this way and that maybe it was genetic because he felt it also. "My dad had this feeling worse than I did. He would procrastinate over things and he has talked to me about it, feeling like a failure because of the procrastination and using drugs and alcohol to blunt that feeling. I think that is why guys put things off, it is fear. It is the sense of letting the people you care about down." Daniel stated that he didn't want to disappoint or fail his family or his parents.

"Do you think that guys who are thirty, living at home, who are labeled as 'failure to launch' types have a fear of failure?" I asked.

Daniel stated that, "Yes, there is fear or maybe even a comfort in small repetitive failures," that these men experience. Ben, who had been listening quietly at that point, added,

"Maybe it's like, how can you fail at something if you don't even try?" "Maybe it is a fear of growing up," Daniel tacked on. "It's knowing that your parents can't do everything for you. People are afraid of the responsibility of being an adult."

"Why?"

"I think it's just that people just want to take the easy way out of everything and it is so much easier to be a kid." "Society has changed," added Max. "America's now lazy. It's just easy not to feel you failed if you never try."

"Yes, your parents will keep you fed and housed," said Daniel, "and guys don't want to give up that safety that they've had their entire life because they are afraid of what is in the real word. It's so easy to stay in the same lanes you've been in your whole life."

"The biggest fear is that if you try too hard and you fail, it would have all been for nothing," said Max. As the men talked, their points about failure made me think of a book I just read called *Atomic Habits,* where the author, James Clear, says that the pain of failure correlates to the height of expectation. "When desire is high, it hurts to not *like* the outcome. Failing to obtain something you want hurts more than failing to attain something you didn't think much about in the first place. This is why people say, 'I don't want to get my hopes up.'"[65]

Daniel pointed out that the biggest fear in humans is change. "We are all creatures of habit. Most people do the same thing every day and they are afraid to jump into a new experience they have never tried. I think people just don't know what's dangerous out there." Max added that he liked change

---

[65]   James Clear, *Atomic Habits: An Easy & Proven Way to Build Good Habits & Break Bad Ones* (Avery, New York, 2018) 263.

and wants to move somewhere new but "I think the danger of life for men is failure."

A Note on Risk-Taking

As I listened to the guys talk about failure and fear of risk, I thought about how it confirmed the research by Jonathan Haidt in his book *The Anxious Generation*.[66] Haidt discuses boyhood without real-world risk. He says that a world with too much supervision and not enough risk is bad for children, but it seems to have a larger impact on boys. Boys used to turn their emotions outward and exhibit more externalizing behaviors—that is, they would engage in more high-risk or anti-social behavior. But around 2010, both sexes showed internalizing behavior like depression and anxiety as they turned their emotions inward. Both sexes now are more like females—they both show more internalizing disorders where they feel that they cannot do anything right. Boys are now taking fewer risks. Haidt believes that keeping kids overly safe in the 80s and 90s, and males' declining social value, led to more of them moving into the virtual world and they have stayed there ever since. I believe this inability to take risks along with other societal factors has led to men increasingly dropping out of society.

Women are Supported, Men are Not

Initially, a few of the men mentioned that women at their college knew more about what they wanted to do and were

---

[66] Jonathan Haidt, *The Anxious Generation: How the Great Rewiring of Childhood is Causing and Epidemic of Mental Illness* (Penguin Press, New York, 2024), 180–185.

"crushing it." But after the discussion about why men are afraid of failure, several of them reflected about why it may be harder for men to push forward and risk failure than for women at college. "Women are much more headstrong about what they want to do but they have someone to fall back on—their families," Max said. "Women get more financial support for college than men." Ben added, "Say you are eighteen and told to leave the house for college or somewhere. Men generally have nowhere to go back to."

Ben looked hesitant at that point to say anymore, lest he look like he was saying something negative about women. This is true of most men I interviewed. They were not used to airing anything that looked like it could be construed as negative about a woman or in favor of a man. I told him that I wanted his honest opinion and asked if he thought men or women were more supported by society in general. "Women, I guess," he said, finally.

"Women are super set on their goals, it is very impressive," Max said.

"Do you think women receive extra support to reach their goals?" I asked.

"I can't answer that directly," said Daniel, "but I think our culture has reached a shift where women are looked after and appreciated just for being themselves, and now it has shifted to where women can do anything men can do. But at the same time, they have their goals confirmed as well as the care of people." Max made a good observation. "Women are cared for and encouraged because they are women. But they are also protected like in the old days, but now they are also told they can do it all."

"Does the old contract still apply to women, that they are to be protected and treated as women used to be, but also told they can do anything a man can do or better, and supported for that choice?" I asked.

"Yes, I agree with that," said Daniel. "The view of what a man should be doing in society is the exact same. But women's view of what they should do has shifted to what a man and a woman should do."

The lack of encouragement, support and resulting fear of failure for men may be why so many men never leave the nest. And it is not just parental support that some men lack. Some studies show that men go to college less often due to a lack of financial aid or scholarships. For example, Richard Reeves points out that "Despite the fact that women have overtaken men in post-secondary education, there are almost no scholarships for men, and virtually none aimed at encouraging them in HEAL"[67] [health, education, administration, and literacy fields].

How Can Higher Education Attract and Help Men?

Next, we turned to colleges and how they could help the average man succeed. We discussed the high rates of women in college (60 percent women, around 40 percent men) and what colleges could do to make it a more welcome place for men. "Many men go to trade schools instead of college to get out in the work world faster and to be in a place where they feel they are not wasting time on courses they don't want," several of

---

[67] Reeves, *Of Boys and Men*, 161.

the guys said. "What are your recommendations for colleges to help men succeed?" I asked.

Ben answered, "Maybe help men gain some experience before they step into trade schools," and Max chimed in, "provide more scholarships for men in trade work in general and in the colleges. Why not set up trade schools in colleges or some way for men to get a degree along with their specialty in a trade?" Most of the frat guys were aware that they had taken a different path in finance or business, but understood that men who had only a high school education or less with a trade degree had a harder time advancing in their fields to management or administration. Many jobs demand a college degree even if it is not necessary for the job. "I think there should be a gateway into the trades via a college degree," said Ben. "It would give guys a better base than they would normally have and more options later on to advance in their trade." Max added, "I see many guys who are going into trades just taking a basically business administration route and then going into one of them. But this is the long way around. College should be more specified."

Ben, who had left the group for a while, came back in and added, "One of the things that pushes people away from college is that you have to take classes that have nothing to do with why you are there. I think that the first two years of college are a complete waste of time." All the guys nodded their heads "yes." "The last two years of college are the only time you start to learn something for the major or reason you went to college two years ago," said Ben. "People have learned that you can get more initially by starting low on the totem pole in a company and working your way up than wasting two years of learning English, history, and science as a business major. In reality, what colleges should be saying is 'you're coming here and choosing this major and for the next four years, you should be focusing on this.'"

Carter came in and sat down, and I asked him how colleges could be more welcoming and attractive to men. "That's a tough question. I don't think it is necessarily that men are not attracted to college. A lot of the jobs you can get with a high school diploma are going to be mostly blue collar jobs. Those jobs have heavily male employees. A lot more men than women see that as an opportunity to make money quicker in the short term but in the long run, these jobs may not pay off as well. There are more options for guys coming out of high school than for girls."

"Why can't women do these jobs such as a mechanic or trade job?" I asked him.

"These jobs are traditionally more male, and women can do them. There is no explaining why women don't do them." Daniel added that these jobs were "more labor intensive and maybe women wouldn't be as excited about jobs like that." I suspect that many women would not like a "dirty job" and prefer to be in an office or place where comfort is more paramount.

Max felt that colleges should help those guys set up for success in the trades via a college degree. "The problem is that you can go much cheaper to a trade or two-year school, so expense for guys is an issue. If the colleges could offer something more beneficial with the college degree, such as how to set up a business in the trades and how to manage a group of welders on an oil rig, it would be better. The four-year degree should offer these men a way to learn skills in addition to their trade, such as welding, to give them the opportunity to advance, not plateau like they might without the college degree."

The guys are correct here that many men without college degrees are plateauing both in terms of wages and opportunities. Why is this happening? In her book, *Second Class*, Batya Ungar-Sargon points out that those without college degrees have been steadily losing ground since the 1970s. The wages of the working class have stagnated due to a number of factors. "Before 1970, the biggest sector of the U.S. economy was manufacturing; a quarter of our nation's wealth was once generated there, where workers got great healthcare, excellent wages and a pension…. Manufacturing meanwhile, [now] makes up just 11 percent of today's economy."[68]

Ungar-Sargon points out that good manufacturing jobs were shipped overseas and immigrants who made up 5 percent of the economy in 1970 make up 13 percent of the economy today, and are willing to do these jobs for less pay than Americans. We now have a knowledge-based economy that emphasizes college. "This emphasis on college turned out to be little more than a sleight-of-hand to disguise the devastating impact globalization meritocracy was having on the American working class."[69] The media and politicians telling us that everyone needs a college degree to deal with this knowledge-based economy are just trying to hide the fact that men's jobs have been shipped overseas. It is much easier to tell men they are stupid and unable to compete with women in this new "knowledge based" economy where women rule.

But it is a world the elite created, in part, I believe to make it easier for women to succeed with "soft skills" and harder for men. Now men are being told that if they don't gain these

---

[68] Batya Ungar-Sargon, *Second Class: How the Elites Betrayed America's Working Men and Women* (Encounter Books, New York, 2024). 12–13.

[69] Ungar-Sargon, *Second Class*, 133.

"soft-skills" like women have, they can't compete. They are supposed to turn to jobs that involve a high "EQ" (emotional intelligence) rather than IQ. But many men aren't buying it and have opted out or found other ways to live their own lives with the skills that they feel fit them. College may or may not be a part of their plan but it seems that schools need to adapt to men's needs just as they have adapted to women's if they want to attract and help more men succeed.

Liberal Girlfriends

Finally, towards the end of the interview, I asked the guys one last time about the politics of the women on campus and more specifically, of their girlfriends. "Are their politics different than yours?" I asked. "Yes," said each guy in turn. Ben stated that the majority of women on campus had liberal views and the majority of men had more conservative views. "How does that affect your dating life?" I asked. All of the men except one had a girlfriend. Daniel said that politics with his girlfriend was "like an elephant in the room, like we both know we are politically different but we don't know how to talk about it. We have viewpoints that are different like the Second Amendment. My dad owns a gun and is sixty-five and knows he is not as strong as he used to be. He wants to be able to protect our home, my mom, stuff like that. My girlfriend's family is very against guns and doesn't believe that guns are necessary in the country at all. We just don't discuss it. It would be a weird topic to discuss. It does not interfere with our relationship."

Carter said he is conservative and his girlfriend is liberal. "I think it is just how we were raised. We talk about politics more often and realize that we are closer to the middle than we originally thought. We keep our emotions pretty calm about it. But it is something in the future that I think about. If I marry this girl and we have kids, there will be a lot of conflicting views on what we tell our kids. These two views can't coexist in a six-year-old's mind. Can we work this out? It concerns me."

The other guys mulled this over as I talked to them about another interviewee who had been called a misogynist and other names for being more traditional. "I get that this would be a fear for men, that politics might lead to disagreements and even divorce. But it is only every four years so maybe it should not be as much of an issue," said Daniel. "What if your value system is just different?" I asked. He replied, "I don't think that is politics. I think that is a question about how we are going to raise our kids. Sometimes politics doesn't match how people actually do things in real life."

I asked Liam, the only guy in the group who was dating different women, what he thought. "The conservative girls I know are happy to have liberal friends but the liberal girls I know are not as accepting. I feel that the girls I go on dates with who are more conservative-leaning want a more muscular conservative man in their life. The more liberal girls want a more feminine man and they 100 percent want a liberal man." "Does this bother you, that the liberal girls have different views?" I asked. "Hmm, no," he said. "I would prefer to have a girlfriend who had similar views to me but I don't think that is a deal-breaker. I think the issue is, if you are unable to have a friend who is different politically, it is ridiculous. My dad is very Republican and his girlfriend is very liberal. They don't fight and keep their views to themselves. His life is different though, because she did not raise me or my sister and they got together later."

All of the men agreed that their concern was about their future kids and how divided politics would affect raising them with a wife with different views. Max said, "It's funny because I think most people when you talk to them are on the same page."

"Do you think social media plays a part in this radical political climate?"

"I think it does and it is also how politics is conducted now," said Daniel. "The two candidates have to be on far sides of the spectrum in order to obtain these votes." "They have to be all the way left or all the way right," said Max. "And they won't get their parties' endorsement. Like if they are a traditional Democrat or someone like RFK Jr., who can't get his party's endorsement because he is not as far left as his party wanted."

Thoughts on Men, Women, and the Government

"If you love freedom, you are now an extremist."

Twenty-one-year-old Max

"Women use the government as the authority instead of a man in the house, now that they don't have one."

Twenty-one-year-old Ben

"Do men and women think differently about the government?" I asked.

"A lot of girls value the aspect of the government taking care of them, said Max. "I think the main difference in the way men and women see the government is that most men could care less about the government taking care of them."

"Yes, definitely," said other men in the room. "Women see the government as some highfalutin thing that should influence their lives," said Daniel. "Men don't trust the government with as many things, they just want the government to set them up for success so they can do stuff on their own and give back in the form of taxes—not a lot, but you know, it is a relationship of give and take." "The risk to be on our own is in our nature. That is why men are afraid to fail, because there is no safety net, but that's okay," said Ben.

"And if you do fail, the government turns against you," said Max. "Say for example, your wife divorces you, then the government comes in and says you owe her money. Or they can come in and take your kids."

"Do you think men value freedom more than women?"

Liam chimed in, "I think women are more empathetic to the general population than men are. They care. This sounds bad, how can I say this? I think women want to care more about how people they don't know feel whereas men care more about themselves being successful. I think this is because society has put more pressure on men to be successful."

"Women care more about themselves emotionally," said Max.

"But is it empathy to say that 'I want the government to come to *your* house to take your gun away,' for example?" I asked.

"I feel as an individual, I wouldn't want the government to have that much control over me," said Ben. Most of the guys seemed to understand where the women were coming from, even though they disagreed with their conclusions.

"I think women are more focused on the empathy of human emotions," interjected Daniel, "like giving people the choice to have an abortion or not. Or I guess they think guns are dangerous but not people. Take immigration. Women support more people coming into our country than men do. Men have a different thought process. Protecting the border is protecting other people's daily lives here whether we see the problems today or not. Men are more likely to think about the next ten or fifteen years. If people keep coming into the country, we are looking at so many people. Women see what is going on now and want to help people in other countries to have a better life."

"Do you think men are thinking through repercussions of what could happen, whereas women are taking a more short-term view with the government?" I asked.

"I think women use the government as the authority instead of a man in the house, now that they don't have one," said Ben, and the others nodded.

DEI

Next, we turned to the problem of DEI (diversity, equity, and inclusion). Liam, who is in finance, added that he believed people should be hired based strictly on their ability to do the job. "If people get a job over me solely because of the color of their skin, I don't think that's right. It makes no logical sense. If they are a better candidate and had a better interview and knowledge, than sure, they deserve that spot over me. There are companies now whose vision is to make DEI seem like a logical and reasonable way to hire people but it makes no sense to me."

"Does this discrimination make you fear for your future?"

"Not yet," he said. "I believe eventually people will go away from DEI. Toyota came out recently and said they are going away from DEI for hiring." Another guy added, "I think companies don't even necessarily believe in DEI but they are too scared to go against the grain because they fear for their own well-being. People are just submitting and not really speaking their own minds on what they believe." "They just go along. It's not right," said Liam.

"Would you speak up yourself?" I asked. "You are speaking up about it right now."

Liam laughed and said, "Yes, but I guess my real name won't be in your book."

We ended the interview and I thought about how these young men's lives would change in the next few decades as I walked back to my car. I can only hope that with the new presidential administration, changes are coming that will help these thoughtful, young men succeed. Or maybe the culture will change in a way that values both men and women, rather than seeing men as a problem to be solved. One can only hope. And coincidentally, a couple of months after the election, the Trump administration is pushing companies to do away with DEI programs[70] and it can't happen soon enough.

The next chapter focuses on middle-aged men whose interviews shed light on how men are dealing with some of the relational and work issues that these fraternity guys are concerned about. I hope that any young men reading this book will pay special attention to what these men have to say and learn from their experiences. As the saying goes "A smart person learns from his mistakes, but a truly wise person learns from the mistakes of others."[71]

---

[70] Breck Dumas, "Trump pushes companies to abandon DEI initiatives — but these businesses won't back down," *New York Post*, January 31, 2025. https://nypost.com/2025/01/31/business/trump-pushes-companies-to-abandon-dei-initiatives-but-these-businesses-wont-back-down/

[71] "Ken Schramm Quotes," *Goodreads*. https://www.goodreads.com/author/quotes/169617.Ken_Schramm

CHAPTER FOUR

Middle-Aged Men Speak Out

"Some men are willing to contort themselves
to avoid making women angry with them."
Psychology Today, *April 2023*[72]

"American men are too tolerant, and it's going to kill them."

Navid, Interviewee from Iran

How are middle-aged men doing these days and what is on their minds? I recently asked Terry Bullman, a world-famous mixed martial artist and instructor who just turned fifty, how he thought men were doing these days. Terry and his wife run a boutique resort in Costa Rica and offer a "Balanced Man Retreat" focusing on martial arts, hiking and breath work to help (mostly) middle-aged men recapture their sense of lost

---

[72] Avrum Weiss, PhD, "Why So Silent?," *Psychology Today*, May 2023, 29.

masculinity and recover from the burnout and stress they encounter in their daily lives. Many of the men that attend are going through a divorce or relationship issue and want a place where they feel accepted and can find fellowship with other men.[73]

I ran into Terry on one of his trips back to the States and he gave me a snapshot of what men in his retreats are concerned about. He made some great points about how little validation men get in a given day. "Men are told not to complain and just to accept whatever is said and keep it inside. Many of the men feel stressed and don't have anywhere to let it out, but in our retreats, we do physical activities initially and build up to breath work and then do check-ins where we see how the guys are *really* doing. No one ever asks men how they feel, they might feel like 'this sucks' about some situation but they can't do anything because they will be seen as weak. Or they are told to act like women. They don't have a healthy view of masculinity."

Terry continued, "Some of the men who come to our retreats have never been hit or punched before so we do boxing the first thing so they can see what it feels like. Many of the men mistakenly think they will automatically turn into Jason Bourne if some dangerous situation comes up but that's not how it works. You have to train over time and be ready for dangerous situations." Just like with physical altercations, today's middle-aged men in the US need to be prepared mentally for the current minefield they find themselves in when it comes to navigating marriage and relationships. Some men I talked with were gut punched by their relationships but others had found

---

[73]   The Balanced Man, https://www.thebalancedman.life/

ways to be successful in a relationship or out of one. Their mental toughness, along with flexibility and forethought, made the difference.

But before we turn to the interviews, let's start with the question, how is middle age defined? Middle age is defined differently according to which source you look at to get your numbers. For instance, the American Psychological Association defines it as around "36 to 64."[74] For this book, I will categorize middle age as roughly forty through fifty-five as this is usually (at least in the past) a time when men are more settled (or not) in their career and relationships and have more perspective to draw on than their younger counterparts. They are struggling with different life patterns that are unique to this age group such as marriage, kids and mid-career transitions. What are some of the issues that men have when reaching the cusp of middle age, that is, the younger side of middle age? To be clear, I don't think that thirty-seven is middle-aged these days but *Men's Health* decided that it is for purposes of their poll.

Men's Health surveyed "530 37-year-old men in the U. S. from December 21, 2020, to January 25, 2021" and found the following:

> *Most guys felt "pretty good" about being 37, but "great" was more elusive. And one in four men leaned toward midlife crisis. In terms of race and income, white men and guys making less than $35,000 were more likely to feel "not great" than*

---

[74] "adulthood," *APA Dictionary of Psychology*, American Psychological Association. https://dictionary.apa.org/adulthood

"great," and overall, white men rated themselves
worse than Black, Asian, and Hispanic men did.[75]

The survey doesn't go into any reason that white men, in particular, feel worse about themselves as they get older, but given the high rate of suicide and depression in white, middle-aged men, it is clear that their mental health is suffering more than other groups. In fact, 69 percent of suicides in 2020 were committed by white middle-aged men.[76]

My guess is that white men are more often than not the butt of jokes, repeatedly told they are no good and that they are the source of all problems, and this has added to their unhappiness. They are always told they are responsible for the ills of society, but given the least amount of assistance or help or even compassion if anything goes wrong in their lives, or if they struggle with depression or other emotional issues. And unlikely to take help even if offered for fear of seeming "unmanly." Few men in general are likely to go for counseling and who can blame them? Therapists are often female or male feminists who think men are the problem, making the men feel worse. Even the American Psychological Association thinks masculinity is harmful[77] and the sexism trickles down to biased therapists who believe that men are always the problem

[75] Max Berlinger and Ben Paynter, "The New Middle Age is 37. Here's How to Make It Awesome," *Men's Health*, April 13, 2021. https://www.menshealth.com/trending-news/a35967798/middle-age-survey/

[76] "KSHB: Suicide Rates High in Middle-Aged White Men," Saint Luke's, September 21, 2022. https://www.saintlukeskc.org/about/news/kshb-suicide-rates-high-middle-aged-white-men

[77] Christopher J. Ferguson, "The American Psychological Association Is Waging War on Men and Boys|Opinion," *Newsweek*, September 22, 2022. https://www.newsweek.com/american-psychological-association-waging-war-men-boys-opinion-1744998

and women are somehow always innocent. This dynamic leads many men to avoid help even if they are open to therapy.

Most of the men surveyed in the men's health poll would rather turn to exercise or alcohol to help with their mental health rather than go to therapy, only 6 percent of men would go to therapy if they had a problem and 7 percent would turn to alcohol. At least alcohol may provide some momentary relief but a therapist is a wild card. Most would use exercise or sex to feel better (33 percent and 23 percent respectively). Interestingly, there was no mention of turning to a friend for help for an emotional issue, which seems to be a good way to destress, and many of the men I interviewed confirmed this. And it's no wonder the men feel stressed or down. The majority of the men in the survey weren't as financially stable as they would like (61 percent). And they were unhappy at home and work:

> *More than 40 percent of men weren't happy with their family life, and, when asked about job fulfillment, more than 50 percent weren't satisfied at work. Men who were in a relationship or had kids were more likely to feel content. But not by much.*

But their relationships were often the sources of their stress with 30 percent of the men being afraid of ruining a relationship. This is their second biggest worry after some unforeseen tragedy or catastrophic event happening to them (36 percent). There was no mention of what this tragic event would be, but I assume that it could have something to do with the pandemic, a divorce or illness.

None of these studies or polls asks about how the anti-male society may contribute to these stresses and depression. But then, why would they, since men are always seen as the source of the problem. It's no wonder so many men are so afraid of angering a woman by speaking up. They know that the culture, the courts, and the media are against them. In turn, so are women. Hence, probably why they are so afraid of ruining a relationship—it is easy to feel that way when men are told their feelings don't matter.

One forty-seven-year-old interviewee told me he tried counseling only to be told that his sexual *needs* didn't matter, and the female therapist confirmed his wife's desire to be left alone. He had no right to ask for anything from her, not even an acknowledgement of their wedding anniversary. He finally stopped talking in the counseling sessions and quit soon after.

Men often keep their mouths shut about any mistreatment they receive just for being male, but in the following interviews I conducted with middle-aged men, it is clear that anti-male sentiment in their relationships, family life, and jobs are sources of stress and confusion. Some of the men walk on eggshells around others but some were more resourceful in their coping mechanisms. Bradley, my next interviewee is one of the more resourceful.

Bradley

"I've never met a drug dealer or violent man that was short of women."

Bradley is a forty-five-year-old registered dietitian living in Queens, New York who contacted me on Facebook to be interviewed. He is savvy about men's issues, having read many of the current articles and books in the field. We met over Zoom and talked for over an hour and a half about his life, and how growing up with a single mom and a mentally ill father affected him and his outlook on sex and dating. We followed up with numerous emails and Facebook messages to clarify his positions on a variety of issues since an hour and a half was not nearly enough.

Bradley described himself as intuitive at a young age and understood that his parents' marriage couldn't last due to his dad's illness. His father left the house when Bradley was thirteen and his younger brother was eight. "My brother was literally hanging onto my dad's ankle as he tried to leave. He had a huge attachment to my dad but I understood that the marriage wasn't viable. My dad was an incurable case. If you put him in a hundred years of therapy, he would not get better. My dad went to Creedmoor [a psychiatric institution in Queens] at one point where he had major depression, anxiety, and even some bipolar disorder.

"My brother is now the spitting image of my dad; he was devastated by the loss and turned to criminality as he got older. He ended up in a juvenile detention center for three years for drug dealing. We had a very different lifestyle. I lived in a very tumultuous household and it was very hard for my mother to deal with my brother. I became a very depressed person after Dad left. My dad was negligent and irresponsible and my brother became the same. I was a body builder and disciplined. My mom was a teacher and very hard working. She was born in Cuba and was also Jewish and my father was Jewish and grew up in the Bronx. Mom was very busy and all of this affected me greatly, especially as a boy."

"How so?" I asked. "I think it depends on a person's constitution. I had a very dictatorial mother. We were very close and people called me a mama's boy but she bent over backwards to help me. This turmoil created a visceral anger in me. Stephen

Baskerville,[78] in his writings, said that fatherless men have this visceral rage. If it were not for my restrained personality, I would have gone in the wrong direction with the amount of rage that I had. When you are raised by a mother who is trying her best... she had to be this way, she was doing a million things, making dinner and she had this boy who wants her attention, you're done. She would say 'go take out the garbage, do this, do that' in a very hostile way. It had a hostile flavor."

"So you felt she wasn't warm?" I asked. "No, it was simply a dictatorial relationship," he replied.

"My mother showed that she did not care about me even though at the time, she did. I was sent to this huge school with 4000 students in Bayside, Queens with so many different demographics and many violent people who had no business being there. I would not want these people around my son or daughter. I had problems at home and I did not fit in at school and got no attention from women. You develop this f**k you mentality. The girls in the school who were the prettiest—the ones that the boys were already looking at, always went for the worst of the males. The message here is that the young guys who get first dibs on women didn't do much work. The male podcasters will tell you to 'improve yourself' to get women but this doesn't work. A good chunk of attractive women are attracted to antisocial behavior."

---

[78] Stephen Baskerville, "Revolt of the Fatherless," *Chronicles: A Magazine of American Culture*, May 2022. https://chroniclesmagazine.org/view/revolt-of-the-fatherless/ See also: Baskerville's website, https://www.stephenbaskerville.com/

Girls Are Attracted to Guys Who Are Low Status

"I have met violent men in my life and I have never met a drug dealer or a violent man that was short of women. I am not saying all women go for these types of men," Bradley stated, "I am saying that many of the sixteen- to twenty-five-year-old women who are the prettiest go for these types of men. Maybe they are not the best quality women but I am sure they are nice to the men they are with. I have known some of these women, who now have dead boyfriends who are not here anymore and now these women are living middle-class lives by thirty or so.

"Male podcasters talk about hypergamy [women gravitating toward high-value men] but what they don't tell you when you are young is that young women *also* go for the low status men. These men can be alpha males though. This is happening in the US and then the decent men are left with the cleanup.

"I have good insight into what the pathologies are since I am from the coast. Much of this anything goes sexual hierarchy started in the cities first and then it moved out to the middle class areas. I saw this behavior with my brother—I was a square but he was the type that just said 'f**k you.' He was never womanless, he always had someone. Even though he had bad habits and was always overweight and I was into bodybuilding, it didn't matter. I think the way that the world treats you is reflective of how you are spoken to at home. I tried to be good to others, altruistic, and wanted to be a good son. But I did not have a dad in the home and I had no one to teach me life skills like how to deal with sex or cope with other men. I was not outgoing and women could read this quickly. I tried to be respectful and did not make the first move. But later, on the dating apps and from women I knew, I found out that some of them did like me and would have wanted me to make a move."

Male Podcasters and Writers Give the Wrong Advice

"You always hear male podcasters or writers telling you to improve yourself to get women, like become wealthy or work out. But this advice makes no sense when fifteen to twenty-year-old guys get women all the time and what did they do to get them? Growing up I saw guys this age getting women by being *who they were*, by being antisocial. They didn't choose to be like that, it is just who they were."

"Do you think the young women change as they get older?" I asked.

Bradley replied, "There is hypergamy, women want high status men but the status does not just come from working on yourself, like men are told. Status is your clout—it could be your looks, your friend circle, gang membership, criminality. The Myron Gaines' and the Rollo Tomassi's of the world [authors mentioned earlier] who tell men to work on themselves, go to the gym, it is not the best advice. Yes, it helps, but the aggressive guys get the women first and then the guys told to work on themselves get what is left. These aggressive men get all the women and they've done nothing. So why would working on yourself help?

"What I don't understand is, when I hear all the stories online from women who say they were manipulated or abused by these men, I say, 'well how is it that these abusive men always have women to manipulate or abuse?' Or I ask the woman if she has no agency and just makes poor choices."

"Do you think women make poor choices?"

"I think some women are excited by the manipulation. Women want a man with an edge. At least that is what some of them tell me. But when you look for that charm or edge, it can be a problem later on."

I asked Bradley more about his education and dating life, and he said that he went to college and has a master's degree in nutrition. At nineteen, he met a girlfriend on a free dating website called AOL Singles. "It lasted two years but that was it. I think that my environment really influenced the way I saw relationships. I hung out at a gym in Bayside, Queens at that age and there was another crowd there that was light-years ahead of me and my friend. The guys weren't bad per se, but they were kind of unambitious types and had an edge to them and would ride motorcycles. These men had their choice of women. We could maybe get the plain Jane next door but there weren't many choices."

Incels and the Black Pill

"I think where you live plays a part in how you do with women. I read men's discussions in online forums and I tell them, 'I don't know where you live, but if you were growing up in Queens in the 90s, you might have been an incel [involuntarily celebate man] yourself.' The diversity of Queens, I think, left some men out in the cold or playing catch-up. You're around rich people and you are around other guys who are lower class but have clout through other means. There are guys who don't fit in either group."

"How would you define an incel?" I asked.

"I am using it in the literal sense, as in a womanless man. I am not using it like some people do as a slur or insult. If a man doesn't have a woman, people say to him, 'Oh, you're strange, you don't like women, you're a misogynist or an incel.' Why don't people stop calling names and think about how these boys or men have been treated or what is happening for them. These slurs cause depression and suicidal thoughts. I agree with the incel crowd—the red pill crowd think that they can hack your way into success with women, but the blackpill crowd believes more in determinism, meaning that raw attraction comes from who the guy is."

Many readers will understand the terms "red pill" and "blackpill" in the men's movement that Bradley is referring to here, but for those who don't, here is a basic Wikipedia definition:

> *The metaphor of the blackpill was first popularized by the incel-related blog Omega Virgin Revolt. In this parlance, being red-pilled means believing concepts like male oppression and female hypergamy, while being black-pilled means coming to believe that there is little that low-status or unattractive men can do to improve their prospects for romantic or sexual relationships with women.*[79]

The problem with "blackpill" determinism is that individual men may feel there is little they can do to have a relationship with a woman, and now that society acts as if a man is a loser if he doesn't, it makes men feel that there is little that can be done or changed. But realizing that a relationship is just one avenue of pursing happiness and self-worth, and that there are others, is an important concept to grasp. Why is it so important that men's worth today is tied up in a relationship with a woman?

---

[79] "Red pill and blue pill," Wikipedia. https://en.wikipedia.org/wiki/Red_pill_and_blue_pill

Men's Worth Is Now Tied Up in Attracting Women

"Years ago, a man didn't need a woman to prove his worth," I added as I continued my Zoom conversation with Bradley. "Men were out doing things, finding their worth in other areas. Now, it seems if a man does not have a woman, people, including the man himself think there is something wrong with him." (And the earlier poll from *Men's Health* bears this out, 30 percent of men are now most concerned about ruining a relationship.) "Why do you think in today's times, men's worth is based on their ability to attract a woman? What has changed?"

Bradley replied, "I think in the old days, there was church and people got married young and there wasn't this whole emphasis on sexual promiscuity. Now, sexuality is unrestrained and anything goes, and people have sex with numbers of people. Sex has become a currency. And there is this 'big man culture.' The man with the most women is the coolest. He's the real man…. I think women will put up with a lot of shit from these types to get one of these high status men."

Dating Sites

"I have to say that I did use the dating websites for a period of time in my twenties and met a lot of women. They seemed to work pretty well in Queens and I think some women found me attractive. My cousin met someone on Tinder." "Do you think the apps work better in the city?" I asked. "The crowd I am around is a biased group. I think we are moderately attractive middle-class people, with good social skills. I think if you are socially astute and can interact with people, you may not be in the top 10 percent, but you will do mildly well on the apps.

"There is a hypergamy with the apps, yes, but I think it is a bit exaggerated because there are still people out there like me who are moderately attractive who have benefitted from them. Women have issues with the apps. But I think a lot of men have a problem too. I don't like using a rating system of one to ten, but my advice would be, if you are a five, find another five or even a four. A lot of men simply want beautiful women and that's a problem. Now with these apps, even the men want to have the so-called hottie. They don't just want to walk around with a normal woman. I don't want to put my fellow man down so I won't."

Bradley is correct here, men (and women) want to punch way above their weight when looking for a date on the apps. In one study looking at the aspirational pursuit of mates in online dating markets, the researchers found "that both men and women pursue partners who are on average about 25 % more desirable than themselves."[80]

Men Put Each Other Down

"Everything now is seen through the lens of women."

"Do men put each other down a lot?" I asked.

"Oh yeah, definitely. They look at the world around them and cannot analyze it. Other men or male activists tell men to 'man up' or 'keep improving.' Well, when does that end? These men will get women on their podcasts and there are thousands of videos asking women what *they* want. It is like the women

---

[80] Elizabeth E. Bruch and M.E.J. Newman, "Aspirational pursuit of mates in online dating markets," *Science Advances*, Vol.4, Issue 8, August 8, 2018. https://www.science.org/doi/10.1126/sciadv.aap9815

have the sexual market in a chokehold. Men put other men down to get to the top of the heap."

"What do you think of Jordan Peterson?" I asked. (He's the psychologist who writes about and advises men and boys.)

Bradley looked annoyed. "I can't stand him. He is another man that puts other men down. He is like a wolf in sheep's clothing. He knows better. He knows what is going on. Men like putting other men down because that is the way you get to the top of the heap these days. They can't empathize with other men. They cannot recognize male disenfranchisement and the deindustrialization of men and they believe that these men as individuals can pull themselves up by the bootstraps. You cannot pull yourself up by the bootstraps in this kind of anarchic system."

I asked Bradley to clarify what he meant by male deindustrialization and disenfranchisement. His points about deindustrialization were similar to what Richard Reeves said about systemic problems causing some of the "malaise" that men are having today. But unlike Reeves or other authors who think that the systemic problems in the US happened organically, Bradley points to a concerted effort to displace men.

Bradley followed up in an email. "Like the rest of us who have been paying attention to men's issues, he [Peterson] is well aware of the trajectory that got us here: decades of decline of manufacturing jobs that ordinary men once had, the shift to a service-based economy, sexual 'liberation'/revolution and all the negative consequences of it, the decline of male academic and financial achievement (as you know, men are now a minority on college campuses, a condition that I do not believe came about organically), and other maladies affecting men (suicidality, despair, addiction).

"I never once have heard Peterson provide any societal solutions for male disenfranchisement, unlike Devlin[81] and Baskerville. Instead he points the finger at men and exhorts them, in a typical Red Pill fashion (he does not identify as Red Pilled), to 'improve' themselves instead of proposing changes to laws, exhorting women to manage their maladaptive sexual proclivities (obviously many don't have them), fairness and termination of favoritism and reinstitution of meritocracy in college admissions, and reintroducing social norms to undo the damage that sexual revolution has done. Instead he provides repetitive psychoanalysis of female sexuality. At times he has lightly and quickly mentioned solutions but he does not nail down on them in the way Baskerville and Devlin do."

Is HEAL the Answer?

I thought about what Richard Reeves said about men going into healthcare fields or teaching, since that is where more jobs are available. I asked Bradley about his work as a dietitian and what he thought of Reeves' solution for men to go into the healing professions (like dietitian, social work, and so on) in order to solve the "malaise" and decline of manufacturing and other jobs for men. "He is giving the wrong advice," Bradley said. "I would give anything if I had known better and gotten the right education and guidance as a young man—I wouldn't be in healthcare. I would have used the scientific and mathematical abilities that I had and my intellect to be an actuary, a physicist or engineer. Reeves and Warren Farrell yield to the female flavor. We should all become like women."

---

[81] The reference is to F. Roger Devlin, author of *Sexual Utopia and Power* (Ministry of Love, 2020).

So, there you go. At least one guy doesn't think HEAL is the answer. But what about younger college men? I asked a professor friend with an account on Sidechat,[82] a college social media site, to put up an informal poll for men asking their opinions about the healing professions. Would they be interested in a career in the healing professions and would a scholarship help them decide to pursue social work, teaching or nursing? Here are the poll questions and what college men said in response:

> *Question 1) Men, would you take a job in one of the Healing Professions (Nursing, Teaching, or Social Work)? There were a total of 79 votes, 48 said Yes, 31 said No. 61 percent Yes, 39 percent No.*

> *Question 2) Do you think men would like these fields? There were a total of 83 votes. 58 said Yes, 25 said No. 70 percent Yes, 30 percent No.*

> *Question 3) What if there were a scholarship available? There were a total of 65 votes. 45 said Yes, 20 said No. 69 percent Yes, 31percent No.*

Maybe the healing professions would be options for men if they felt welcome in these fields and if a scholarship was available. However, this is a college sample of men and may not reflect what non-college men would say about these professions. The fraternity guys I interviewed in person did not want to go into these fields either but did think scholarships might help.

---

[82]   Sidechat app. https://apps.apple.com/tn/app/sidechat-° ° /id1591988276

That said, there are not many scholarships or money for men to go into these fields at all. Reeves states in his book that the Society of Women Engineers has a staff of thirty-six and an annual expenditure of $12 million dollars, while the American Association for the Advancement of Men in Nursing has no employees and an annual income of $183,000.[83] Given this information from Reeves, it seems that women in STEM get all kinds of support. Men in nontraditional fields? Not so much. But enough about the healing professions, let's go back to Bradley's interview and how he met his wife.

Finding the Right Woman and Advice

"How did you finally meet your wife?" I asked towards the end of the interview with Bradley. "I was single and went to the Plenty of Fish website[84] where we met." "Are you happy?" I asked. "Yes. She knows all my views and how I feel." They have two children and his interest now in the men's movement is to help his kids, one of whom is a son, to lead better lives than he did. "What advice would you give to other men to find a good wife like you married?" I asked. "I think it is harder than when I was younger. I'm forty-five and got married around thirty-four, thirty-five, which is late I think. I met her at thirty. I would advise younger men to educate themselves like I did. They should read Stephen Baskerville's work and that of F. Roger Devlin. You need to understand the current landscape. I would say to men that yes, they should improve themselves but you cannot change the way that women are acting now. Become socially savvy, get on a dating app, which has its problems, but

---

[83]   Reeves, *Of Boys and Men*, 158.
[84]   Plenty of Fish. https://www.pof.com/

it's there. I want to start my own website and help other men to do well also."

I asked Bradley to tell me more about his wife and why he married her in a follow-up email. Here is his response:

I met my wife when she was 24 years old.

Here are the reasons I chose her:

I could tell that she was not what my friend and I call a "professional girlfriend," that is, a woman who had "boyfriend" after "boyfriend" from age thirteen to 30. She did not lead an overly-socialized life, the sort that I described to you that I witnessed amongst some of my peers at a young age in which the young women were seemingly constantly around men in cliques in which everyone is sampling everyone. I did not want a woman who went through a series of thrilling relationships and then sought me for stability after them all.

She made it clear in the beginning of the relationship that she wanted to be a mother and that her foremost priority in life would be motherhood. And now I can see that considering she bends over backwards for our children. She is very interested in family life and a healthy social life, and believes spending time with friends and family is important....

My wife is extremely caring towards me, and she showed me so in the beginning of the relationship.

She supports me in all that I do, spoils me with gifts, makes food for me (although I do the majority of cooking simply because I enjoy doing so), takes care of me when I am ill, and grooms me (as I said, she is a hairstylist).

She is also handy and knows how to fix things around a home due to being raised by her carpenter father. She makes a sizable vegetable and flower garden in our backyard every summer.

We have the same values and outlook on life and consider marriage and child raising serious businesses. We have a very dim view on divorce, except for serious, unforgivable transgressions. We do not look at marriage as simply two lovebirds residing with one another.

The men who seem happiest in marriage have a wife who, from the beginning was good to them, and who had similar values. My next interviewee was also fortunate enough to find a wonderful wife, and like Bradley, he understands that the odds against American men (and in other countries as well) are numerous and require not only luck but a clear idea of what is important to them in life and in a spouse.

Navid

"Women have more power than men in the US."

Navid was my next interview in this age group. Unlike the other men I had talked to so far, he was foreign born and English is his second language. He is from Iran and came to the US at the age of twenty-six. He is fifty, married, and living in Orange County, California, but spends part of the year in Tennessee. I chose his story because the patriarchal society he came from gives him the perspective to see clearly both sides of living in a male versus female-dominated culture, and how a female-centered culture affects the mental health of men.

In the US, we constantly hear about the "patriarchy," but Navid *actually* lived under one—one that put people in jail if they did not go along with the program, or worse. He did not approve of the patriarchal society he was from, but he is also very aware that his new country is female-centric and that men are not treated very well as a result. He certainly is not bothered by strong women, as he is married to a successful entrepreneur who came with him to the US from Iran and is running a thriving beauty business here. He is a successful realtor.

They are both Zoroastrians (a very old Iranian religion) which is a religious minority in Iran; they were discriminated against in their country because they were not Muslim. Both Navid and his wife were able to get religious asylum in the US when they were in their twenties. Over the past twenty-plus years, Navid has witnessed men's relationships in the female-centered American society he now calls home, and gave me an account of his findings. His descriptions of the current state of married American men are both sad and accurate.

"Women have more power than men in the US."

"What do you mean?" I asked him.

"Well, let's take divorce. The courts almost always give rights to the woman here in the US. And the women here get married and then they just say, 'Hmm, aw, I don't like him.' I don't know if they just don't like the guy or if they cheat, but I have noticed that the women, they leave the guy and get remarried.

The men they leave get demoralized and he just thinks 'okay, I guess I am no good anymore.' I know friends this happened to but they did not want to talk about it. It was their wife that took off. What I don't get is, after the divorce, the men these women left become friends with the ex even after the woman cheated. Where I come from (in Iran), that's a big no-no—once you cheat, that's it. Even my uncle here in the US still sees his ex-wife; she was American and cheated on him. Now, he will just say she is coming by to visit. What is that about?"

In contrast, I asked Navid what happens when a couple divorces in Iran. He stated that when you get divorced in Iran, the separation is more final, but even there the man must pay out or give something to the woman if they divorce. "There is a promise that if you get divorced, the man will pay the woman something like twenty gold pieces." "What happens if a woman cheats in Iran?" I asked. "They get divorced or stay together. However in rare cases, especially in rural areas, she gets stoned (court order and there should be three witnesses) unless the husband pardons her."

"You mentioned that in the US many American women cheat and then just become friends with their ex. What happens in Iran when a couple divorces?"

Navid answered, "In general, they leave each other and there will be no more contacts unless there are children involved." "You said he has to pay her some gold pieces. Why is that and does he pay it if she cheats on him?"

"It could be gold or anything valuable like a house or even money (cash). It's an obligation that a husband would support the wife. It even could happen while they're still married. The wife may want gold or the house or whatever they agreed on.

And yes, she can get it even if she cheats! It's called Mahr. Every Muslim country is different.

"But here in the US, women can destroy men. They can accuse a man—remember what happened to Brett Kavanaugh? And it seems like women here live with a man, they say he raped them, get a lawyer and destroy him. It is right out of a Soviet book. They can accuse somebody and take them to court without any proof."

"Where does this happen?" I asked. "This happens a lot in politics," he stated.

When I asked if our culture makes men feel good or bad, Navid responded "bad." "How so?" I asked.

"When I go to public places like the grocery store, I notice women talking down to their husband or boyfriends. They are constantly nagging them saying 'I told you to do this or that' and the guy either doesn't respond or tries to explain himself, you know. 'Well honey, I did it because'...or he probably just agrees with her or huffs and puffs. The woman always has the last say.... For a while, the woman will probably like it, thinking 'I am the winner' but then the woman will think he is a wuss and they will get divorced. Every day the woman puts the man down."

I asked Navid why he thought women do this to men— "why do they put them down?" His answer was simple but straightforward and honest. "Because they can." He added, "the media, for the most part, is against men."

Luckily, Navid does not have to deal with these putdowns in his own marriage, but he realizes he is one of the lucky ones. "My wife is in the top 5 percent of women." Navid realized early that a good marriage for a man starts with a supportive wife and one that he can talk to without feeling that he will be abandoned or ridiculed. He described to me a time when he lost some money in an entrepreneurial venture. "I was drinking and afraid to tell my wife because I didn't want to disappoint her. She figured out that something was wrong and when I told her I had lost the money we invested, she was upset but let me know that we would work through it and that it was only money. That brought me a lot of relief and I quit drinking to cover the pain. I am so glad that I have someone like that who understands."

But happens when you don't have that supportive spouse? My next interviewee, Charlie, filled me in on how he dealt with an unprincipled and mentally unstable wife in his first marriage, and why it is so important for men, if they decide to marry, to marry wisely.

His story is a bit long and intense but bear with me. It is an important lesson for men who have been psychologically conditioned to believe that they must care for and protect women no matter how much pain it causes them. This unshakable conditioning, whether it starts with an addictive mother or from societal pressure to provide "as a man"—or both—is important to understand in order to avoid a difficult relationship like the one described next.

Charlie

"My brother drank himself to death...he basically married the same woman I did."

Charlie is a tall, charming man in his early fifties who is dedicated to his current wife and three amazing boys. He describes himself as "wanting to be a good husband, a good dad, and a good provider and predictable." He is a chief financial officer at a software company, and moved to Tennessee from Atlanta to take the new job. His life looks idyllic now, but it was a long road to get to where he is today, a road that no man should have to go down. His first wife almost destroyed his life, had him arrested and left him homeless, and it took him a long time to get his life back on track.

His story began in a small Midwest town where he grew up with a father he described as "an asshole" who didn't get along with people—and he found out later that his dad was a serial cheater. He stated his mother was "definitely an alcoholic" who he found out was also a cheater, and his parents divorced when he was around twelve. His one sibling was a brother who was in the Air Force but in 2019, "he drank himself to death." When I asked Charlie what happened, he stated, "he basically married the same woman I did."

Before we get to Charlie's first wife and what went wrong, let's turn to how he described his mother. Why is this important? Because how he felt about his mother played a part in his choice of a wife, and may have led him to be unable to leave even when his wife was clearly abusive. His father he could dismiss as an "asshole," but it is difficult to dismiss the woman who gave birth to you. As an adult child of an alcoholic, it is common to marry someone who is also an addict, and to hold on to that relationship because of a deep-seated fear of abandonment.[85]

"My mother said if you ever come into money, act like you've always had it. She thought people who had money were posers, but she always wanted money but she never had it. She

---

[85] Buddy T, "Characteristics of Adult Children of Alcoholics," *Very Well Mind*, updated April 28, 2024. https://www.verywellmind.com/common-traits-of-adult-children-of-alcoholics-66557

was a great example of someone who went into massive debt for any bling she could find. When she died in 2005, she had huge credit card debt for jewelry. She was a self-medicating alcoholic, obese, drug addicted. She used any drug that a magazine told her to use. She went over to Mexico to get stuff. She would get opioids, or whatever she could. She finally died of a brain stem stroke."

Charlie described having problems with having money or buying himself things because he felt that he might be one of those "posers" like his mom talked about. Yet he would lavishly turn to giving his first wife things because he thought that is what a good provider did. Or maybe because he wanted to provide all of the things his mother was unable to get in a legitimate way. Whatever the reason, his tolerance and acceptance of his wife's intolerable behavior almost put him in jail.

He met his wife when she was seventeen and they married when she was nineteen and he was twenty-four. "I met her at the mall when I was walking around with my brother. I was with UPS and would travel to see her in Arkansas, but then I was transferred to Nashville. I was going to leave and it was a very emotional time. I had always been in long-term relationships and what happened is, I got scared of being alone and I rushed a proposal."

Right away, Charlie knew he made a mistake. "Her story was that she was working at the mall and wanted to go to cosmetology school. I was on a track with UPS and had a good salary and good benefits and a career in front of me, so I needed companionship and she needed security, I guess, and right after I made the proposal, I was like 'what have I done?' But I figured this was just a natural reaction that many people would have to commitment. I was leaving town to move to Nashville and she was upset. I think it was emotional. I think I proposed because she was upset and I didn't want to be alone. It was an emotionally charged situation and once you put it out there [the proposal], you really can't take it back."

I asked him why he thought he couldn't get out of it. "I thought about it a lot, but that's my personality. I made this decision, I pulled the call and I had to live with it. It wasn't exactly that sterile, it was more like, this is part of an obligation. You are a man, and you have offered and you can't go back on your word."

"What is a man?" I asked Charlie. "Well, people depend on you, if you have a family and you say you are going to do something, you have to do it. You can't back out on it, especially if it is a large commitment. But If you are married, you get something out of it—you get taken care of in a way that you would not do it for yourself. But that was my next marriage with my wife now. But not then.

"Anyway, me and my first wife Kiera moved to Nashville and she worked at a timeshare. In 1998, my first son was born and that's when it went downhill. We wanted kids right away because she had endometriosis. And then the drama started to build around her health and everything else. In late 1998, we had a friend of my brother's that moved to Nashville with his girlfriend and they had a lake house and we went up there a couple of times. Kiera started getting to know the guy and started a relationship with him. I found out the old school way—getting phone records—and I saw she was calling this person. I called the number and the guy answered. At this point, I realized there were other instances where she lied to me and hid things. In 2000, we moved to Atlanta, and we went on a cruise just us for three or four days, and one of the nights I went to bed and she stayed out hanging around and I woke up and no one was there. I wandered around and found her with a guy and she started a relationship with a guy she met on a cruise ship.

"Another time she went to see friends in Ohio and she didn't answer her phone or take my calls or text message. At that point I started building a case, this is what she did, and I documented it.

"She would write in her diary with her name and this other guy's last name and I'm thinking 'what is all this teenage stuff?' We went to counseling in Atlanta. We stayed together for another ten more years. She got pregnant with twins and she lost them during that time, and she was doing drugs like antidepressants, and then she got pregnant with our second son. After he was born, she was looking for more pills from doctors and drinking alcohol with them. I was the only one taking care of the kids. I would go to work, come home, cook and clean, and put the kids to bed."

At this point, I asked him if Kiera reminded him of his mom to which he replied, "my mom wasn't angry, she would give you everything she had. If we needed anything, she would go into debt to get it. She would write bad checks, whatever she could do to give us what we wanted." It seemed that Keira wanted Charlie to give *her* everything she wanted, without a thought to his feelings or how he would get these things. It threw his life into turmoil.

"Keira wanted to get a farm in Mississippi, but I had no way to make a living there and I had already bought her the half a million dollar house, the car.... She would have some plot or scheme that always seemed plausible and I was dumb enough to fall for it. For example, she went to rehab for months and she met a guy in rehab. On my birthday, she got all this stuff together for him for a gift basket and I am like 'but it's my birthday.' She told me he was in need of help for his addiction and I thought, 'what help can she give, she is addicted to drugs and didn't even finish rehab.' Another time, she told me she was going to Mississippi to stay with her dad, but she took all the pots and pans with her. She was staying with a guy she met on Facebook. At this point I had had enough." Apparently, he hadn't as he gave her another chance when she got home and they stayed married until 2010.

What finally broke Charlie was when his wife told her mother that he had pushed her down the stairs and told authorities that he was an abuser. At the time, the family lived in Georgia where domestic abuse (against women only) was taken very seriously. "Fortunately, for me, she left a trail of stupidity. She would write her mother with a picture of her bruised leg after she had fallen down the stairs while drunk and say, 'look what he did to me.' But she would send me the same picture and say 'haha, I fell down the stairs.'" She later took the boys and said she was going to her mom's house and left. Charlie was concerned when he couldn't figure out where she was and he found out she was at her mom's boyfriend's house.

When Charlie drove up to the mom's boyfriend Mike's house, Mike informed him that Kiera had cuts on her and she had called the police. "Mike told me to leave so I went home and I saw a knife on the counter that Kiera had used to cut herself. She told all of her friends and family that I had done this and that I was an addict." Charlie was smart enough to scrape all of her Facebook and email messages. He moved all of his money and credit cards and shut some cards down. "I told her she was a liar. She said she did lie, but that the outcome would be the same. She said to give her a divorce or she would drag my name through the mud. Later, I was sitting at home and I heard a knock at the door. It was a cop. My wife had reported me to a special victims unit and the police were there to remove me from my house. I was told to get my things and get out. She got temporary custody of the boys and I was homeless."

Charlie's story does have a happy ending. He was able to prove that his wife was lying using text and photos he had saved from her. He even scoured Facebook and social media and found data that helped prove his innocence, and asked family members if they had texts or emails that might help him. He finally did get a divorce and later, custody of his kids. He remarried an understanding, kind woman who loved him and his children, and they later had a child together.

But even with a happy ending, Charlie's earlier situation should serve as a warning to men that in twenty-first century America, an unstable woman's word is all it takes to lose your freedom, your livelihood, and even your children. This is why it is important when a man feels that his marriage is abusive to stand up for himself and get legal counsel or help before it is too late. The big takeaway from Charlie's first marriage is that if you feel you are being set up in your marriage for a domestic violence charge or other charges, record your conversations and save any texts or photos that you feel will clear your name if you are accused unfairly.

Freedom is important to many men, and my next inter-viewee, Mark, is an independent guy who has never been married and likes to come and go as he pleases. His life is very different from Charlie's, and though he would like to be cared about and loved by a woman, he is not willing to compromise or change his life in response to a woman's needs. Or maybe he can't. It is hard to say.

Mark

"Men want to feel comfortable."

Mark was indeed different than some of the other men I interviewed. What was different was that, unlike the younger men or other middle-aged guys, he was a man going his own way, even if he did not really describe himself as such. He mentioned wanting to find a woman to marry or hang out with, but his actions showed him more unwilling than most men to compromise or change his behavior in order to live with a woman. Or maybe he was incapable.

He showed up at my office door on time and seemed talkative, though not overly so. He is fifty-four, good looking, and never married. I asked him what he thought would make a good men's center, and he stated that he thought it would be men who were peers sharing feelings and "commiserating with each other." I asked what "commiserate with" meant, to which he replied, "I guess figuring out what is going right in your life and what is not. It can be helpful, I guess, to have other peers to talk to." Mark said he has many male friends, around twelve, that he feels comfortable with and who would be there for him. "I knew these buddies from high school. I can call them and they can call me if there is a problem."

"Would you talk to friends about your relationship with a woman?" I asked. He did not reply directly to the question but stated, "Well, mostly my hang-up has been, at least I have been told, that I don't share. It is not by my choice that I am not married. I have had several relationships where I guess I went through the relationship and thought I could spend the rest of my life with them. But the relationship gets stagnant. My current girlfriend told me that I need to be more interested in her and say things like 'How is your day or something.' I guess I get that kind of feedback from women. I guess it's me is what I am trying to say.

"I think part of it is I don't like to share my feelings. I don't think about intimate things, so if someone asked me about them, I would have to sit and gather my thoughts. I assume women think more about these things. I have a friend, Connor, that I talk to, and I met up with him and my girlfriend, and she commented to him jokingly I guess that I am a closed book. My friend just said, 'this is how Mark has always been.' I am not against sharing my feelings. I suppose I don't spend a lot of time analyzing things. I would say most of my friends would say I am very even-keeled. It is hard to get me upset. I am just not a very emotional person. I don't feel things very deeply."

That said, it did not appear that Mark was convinced he did not feel deeply, adding that he has had tragedy in his life that was very emotional. "What was that?" I asked. "My mom died unexpectedly in 1996. She was getting a hysterectomy which should have been a routine day operation, but she never came home. That profoundly affected me. I was around twenty-seven at the time, and me and my mom were very close. My little brother was only fifteen and my dad was not that involved due to work. I went home to help my dad and brother a lot. Me and dad did not interact much. I am a lot like him; he was unemotional too, I guess. I was the youngest of five and then my baby brother came along. Now that my sisters and me are caretakers for my dad, they say he is more social and will talk on the phone with them for an hour. With me, the conversation lasts for one minute. He just tells me everything is 'fine.'"

"Do you want to be in a relationship?" I asked. "I feel like I want to be in a relationship. I do stuff with my girlfriend like help her clean her rug that the dog messed up. I like being around someone else to do things for and to do things with. I love helping people. I care a lot, I just don't share. Several girlfriends have told me that I need to talk when I just put on a movie or something." "Do you have trouble knowing what to say?" I asked. "I will talk about an article or something I read, but me or my girlfriend don't have that much to say about our day. I don't really tell her I care about her but I do tell her I love her. Saying I care about her is something I should do, I guess." "What would *you* like to do?" I asked.

At this point, Mark stated that he felt a little lost. "I am not good at relationships. I have never mistreated a girl or been an asshole. It is more that I have been told by girls that I am a closed book and they are not getting the emotional attachment they need. They don't feel like I care, they don't get the validation from me that they are important, that their lives are important. I would like to have a good and healthy relationship so I should learn these things. But the way I am, I go to work and go through my day and I don't sit and think about my relationship. I don't know why, I don't have an explanation."

Mark doesn't like to text much with the women he is involved with, but seemed more enthusiastic about texting with his guy friends about fantasy golf, mainly on the weekends. He mentioned going out to play actual golf with some friends soon. "It is just a struggle to validate and communicate in a relationship constantly. Maybe it is just that I have been a bachelor all of my life." "Do you like being a bachelor?" I asked. "I kind of do. I like doing my own thing and decompressing in my own way. Sometimes a woman you are dating doesn't get that. I dated someone for a while who was too clingy and she would just show up at my house. I was coming home at the end of a work day and I just needed to decompress. I ended the relationship. I like a lot of alone time. I don't sleep over with women during the week. My own space is important to me. I would be apprehensive about living with someone. But I never wanted to be a bachelor. I just never met anyone who could make it through the steps of the relationship to marriage. And honestly, talking about feelings all of the time and relationships is just not my way."

And indeed, this lack of need to analyze relationships is common to many men, and is not necessarily pathological in the way that women and "experts" see it. Although I did not do any psychological testing with the men I interviewed, I had Mark take an online version of the Myers-Briggs test, which categorizes people into different personality types.[86] His responses to the questions on the MB showed him to be a type which is described as "needing dedicated alone time to recharge their energy after socializing with others. This alone time is what allows these personalities to reestablish a sense of their own identity – in other words, to reconnect with who they truly are."[87] He is also introverted, assertive, and interested in the here and now, and not so much in the future, and showed a need for personal space. "They are action-oriented and tend to

---

[86] Better Help Editorial Team, "Understanding Your Personality Type With A Free Myers-Briggs Test," BetterHelp, updated February 14, 2025. https://www.betterhelp.com/advice/general/why-you-should-take-a-free-online-myers-briggs-test/

[87] Adventurer, ISFP Personaility, https://www.16personalities.com/isfp-personality

show their care and concern through action rather than discussing feelings or expressing sentiments."[88]

Individualism and autonomy from a man is frowned upon in our society these days. In the past, people saw these traits as normal. Now society views men through a female lens that says men are supposed to be able to see things from the female perspective. This means providing the type of emotional life and assistance in the home that *she* needs while also providing assets, support and a high income. Many men I interviewed, like Mark, mentioned comfort at home as a reason for a relationship, and when they felt discomfort from pressures they feel they cannot meet, they tended to retreat or their partner retreated from them. Thus, men like Mark are not going to have an easy time finding a woman willing to take a man who is not willing to step up and provide the things that are now necessary in the twenty-first century dating market. His current girlfriend recently broke up with him, citing the "closed book and inability to take steps toward living together." There may come a point where Mark may feel it is worth it, but he may also love his comfortable life and freedom as a bachelor more.

That is not to say that men like Mark do not have their issues. It is hard to engage with a man who is only interested in the here and now, and is individualistic to the point of not trying to meet another person's needs in a partnership. Personal space can be a good thing, but taken to an extreme, there may be no room in one's life if they desire mainly to be alone.

That said, it is also possible that some men today, like Mark, are more interested in leading a comfortable life without

[88] Kendra Cherry, MSEd, "ISFP: The Artist (Introverted, Sensing, Feeling, Perceiving)," Very Well Mind, updated July 19, 2024. https://www.verywellmind.com/isfp-introverted-sensing-feeling-perceiving-2795991

a woman than they are in changing themselves to be in a relationship. The Myers-Briggs test can help you understand your own traits and get a snapshot of what kind of person you are and how to work with, rather than against, your personality type. Then you can make a more informed decision about how to proceed in the dating world. If you would like to see what your personality type is, you can just google "free Myers-Briggs test," take the test, find out your type, and read up on your traits. It often helps to have insight into how you view the world and how you perceive other people and relationships. In midlife, it is still possible to learn more about oneself and turn your middle years into a more fulfilling chapter, whether with a relationship or without one.

My next interviewee, Kevin, had both—he was married and divorced, was involved with a previous girlfriend who had his second child, has been alone and now has a girlfriend. He was referred to me by some of his clients who thought he would make a great interview because he has sage advice for other men and for their sons. Kevin owns a wellness business and cheerfully agreed to be interviewed.

CHAPTER FIVE

Kevin Speaks Out

I met Kevin at his therapy office. He welcomed me in and told me to have a seat in his waiting room that contained several comfortable recliners. What I thought would be a one or two hour interview turned into almost four hours, hence the stand-alone chapter to share his perspectives on men, love, kids, and life. Kevin is a forty-seven-year-old black man who started our discussion with the lack of services for men at church. "When I started going to church with my now ex-wife, I noticed that there were always programs and functions for women. It's the women's conference this or the women's club meeting for that but I would rarely hear about anything for men. It was strange. This was a long time ago at a small Baptist church. The pastor was always asking for cash and my wife once gave a thousand dollars there without asking me! It was a hustle." I wondered why Kevin started out with his feelings about church, but by the end of our interview, I understood the importance of it in his life and what it symbolized—that the average man's needs are being left out of not only religious organizations but in the society at large.

Dad and His Early Life

I asked Kevin to tell me about himself and he shared early thoughts about his dad, who was a negative role model but taught him a lot about life. Kevin was born in Tennessee, then lived in New York State, and came back to Knoxville. His parents were divorced and his grandmother took him in, along with his brother and sister, while his mother went back to school in Florida. His dad wasn't around at all when Kevin was growing. up. "That's a whole other thing," he joked. "He is the main reason I am where I am at in terms of making choices and decisions in life. This is why I am telling you all this, to show you how I came to be the way I am in life."

"My mother never dogged him out. She just told me 'you'll see.' My dad was one of the best musicians I've ever seen. He had sixteen kids. My mom was the only woman he ever married. My dad just had his last kid a few years ago and he's in his sixties now. He's just not really a very good person. I worshipped the ground he walked on when I was a kid and would go to the churches he played music at to see him. But my dad was abusive to my mom—they divorced when I was three. My dad hurt me once when I was young and then mom left. After she went to school in business, she went to work at a company in New York. I went to stay with my dad at that time in Tennessee and he left me with his mom, my grand-mother. He had another family and was hardly around. I was like a nurse to his mom, who was sick at the time and I was just like six or seven. I cooked, cleaned and helped her. Dad was basically a user.

"One day my mom came to get me. Dad was mad, went ballistic, and he hit me with the edge of a bottle. Ironically, he was a police officer for work at that time, and when mom said she was going to call the police, he said, 'I am the police.' After this incident, I didn't see Dad again but three or four times maybe. He saw me once at a pool in Blount County while he was riding motorcycles with his friend but did not acknowledge me—and I was done." The next time Kevin saw his dad, he was twenty-one and went to see his grandmother [his dad's mom] who was sick. His dad was there and said to him, 'if you got something to say, say it.'

"I lost it. Punched my dad square in the face and whupped on him for a good five minutes. My girlfriend at the time pulled me off of him. I made sure not to turn my back on him and got in my truck. Dad started shooting at it. Years later, Dad apologized to me and said, 'I just want to be your dad.' I laughed and said, 'look man, I'm thirty-something years old, that's a wrap.' I don't hate the man, I literally don't know him. One day he sent me a friend request on social media and because I didn't answer it as quickly as he wanted, he rescinded it. Another time, he told everyone off in the family on social media and I haven't talked to him in over ten years.

"I have two boys now. One is seventeen with my first wife and I have an eight-year-old with an ex-girlfriend. I get my younger son all the time; he is a tremendous athlete and a gymnast." Kevin was also an athlete when he was younger and played football in high school. He was recruited to play for several large Southern universities, but his mother got cancer his senior year in high school and he stayed home to take care of her.

Sex and Intimacy Were Rare

He was married his first and only time in 2004 to a woman he met at a media business in Knoxville who was four years older than he was. "She was smart, had a masters and got a PhD and is now a professor. I am not one of these guys intimidated by a smart woman. 'I'm not competing with her,' I tell people. Her accomplishments just make me look good. She helped me go to massage therapy school." I asked what happened to his marriage and Kevin laughed. "I always tell people, you don't know what you don't know. I love my ex-wife. I did not know who I was at the time and I overlooked certain things. Everything was great when it started but the moment I said, 'I do,' there was a switch. Sex at that point was non-existent. I didn't understand that my love language was touch and acts of service. She was a person who did not communicate well. She was better at writing. Here's an example. It was our anniversary. I went out and got her flowers. I come home and I think to myself 'she forgot our anniversary.' I took her downtown for dinner. We did not say anything to each other, it was weird. I was that husband who did everything, you know. I would get up and get our son ready for school. Her job was to get him to bed. After she put him to bed, I thought we could at least talk about how we made it another year. But she ate ice cream in the kitchen and did not even come upstairs. I'm thinking, 'what are we doing here?' She said she had postpartum depression or something when I asked her what was wrong, but I think we were just so different. I could trust her though in other ways, so I stayed."

But the sex and intimacy continued to be a problem. "Was it ever good between you?" I asked. Initially Kevin said "no," but then amended, "I guess it was okay. But for me, she just wasn't willing to try to get better as a lover. I can count on one hand the number of times we had sex our first year of marriage—four." At that point, I am thinking, "What a saint!" But Kevin did not seem to think that this was an intolerable situation for most men—it was just that "physical touch" was important to him.

He continued, "I asked her what could we do to save the marriage. She basically said 'nothing.' I saw her diary one day sitting out, I wasn't trying to pry but I picked it up and it said 'I don't understand why my husband wants sex so much. If there was pill I could take, I would so he would just leave me the hell alone.' It sounded like I was bugging her. Okay, I'm thinking, I'm blocking any advances from other women at this time, you're my wife, and why is this happening? It's not normal. I'm twenty-eight, not fifty-eight. What are we doing?" He did admit that later in the marriage, there was infidelity on his part since his wife wanted no or little contact with him. "After the infidelity, that's when she asked me for a divorce." People often attribute men's infidelity to men just being men, but for Kevin, his inability to connect emotionally or sexually with his wife led him to feel neglected. This is common for many men who cheat. They often feel unable to get their needs met emotionally by their wives. This is the exact opposite of the stereotype, that women are looking for an emotional connection and men are simply looking for a sexual one. Men like to be appreciated and feel that they are making a woman happy.[89] Without

---

[89]   M. Gary Neuman, *The Truth about Cheating: Why Men Stray and What You Can Do to Prevent It* (John Wiley & Sons, New Jersey, August 1, 2008).

this respect, it is hard to feel wanted. In addition, Kevin's wife rarely had sex with him, and it finally led not only to infidelity but divorce.

"My wife had talked me into quitting a job I had at the time as a supervisor making good money and staying home to take care of our son. So when she asked me to leave our house, I pretty much lived in my car. The house was both of ours but I am not one to argue so I left. It wasn't like I didn't try; I asked her over and over to try to make it work. We even went to counseling before the infidelity on my part to see if we could make it work."

Counseling Made It Worse

"The counselor was...awful." Kevin sighed as he said this, as if the experience was still a recent bad memory instead of something that had occurred over ten years ago. "Honestly, the counselor never saw any fault with anything my wife did. We went to marriage counseling and unfortunately, we had signed up for twelve sessions. I would own my stuff in the sessions but I feel like the counselor [a woman] was more like an advocate for my wife than for both of us. She wasn't even trying to help us. For example, I would tell the counselor touch was important to me and the counselor would come up with a reason it shouldn't be an issue. So shoot yeah, she was obviously partial to women. It pissed me off because it justified everything my ex-wife thought—that I was wrong to want anything. 'This is bullshit,' I thought. I told the counselor about my wife forgetting our anniversary and not wanting to even talk on that day and the counselor was like 'she doesn't have to talk to you.' And I'm like, "What the f**k?'" "Do you think she was some type of feminist therapist?" I asked. "I think so, I really believe that. During those twelve sessions, there was never a time anything was in my favor. By the last four sessions, I just didn't say shit. I would just sit there." I told Kevin about polls showing that few men want to go to therapy, and asked him if this female-focused treatment was one reason men didn't feel it would help.

Kevin remarked that even a female friend told him if he went to marriage counseling again to only get a male therapist. "I guess therapists are people too and they go through the same problems. God forbid they see something in you that reminds them of what they went through." I explained to Kevin that part of being a good therapist is to understand your own issues and not to take your frustrations out on your patients. We have whole generations of women-first therapists (they can be female or male) who have no clue how to treat men or who treat them as the problem and act as if they have no right to ask a woman for anything. (This is not to say there are not good therapists out there. There are, and in the appendix, I will explain what to look for if you are seeking counseling as a man. However, experiences like Kevin's are common and now that about 76 percent of therapists are women,[90] the problem is getting worse.)

Something Better Was out There

"All I left with was 50/50 custody of my kid."

"During our divorce, her lawyer kept telling me she wanted this or that, she didn't want to give up any of her 401k. 'Okay,' I said. She wanted the house and I gave her that even though it

---

90 Yitz Diena, "Therapist Statistics And Facts: How Many Are There?" *ambitions*, February 25, 2025. https://www.ambitionsaba.com/resources/therapist-statistics

was ours. I didn't care, the only thing I cared about was my son. She moved to Virginia when my son was four and I drove back and forth. I put so many miles on my car, I was burning up the road. I wanted to be there for my son."

"How did you become such a good dad without a role model?" I asked. "I knew there was better out there. I found that out when I lived in New York as a kid. We lived in the projects in the 1980s which were very nice. But it was the crack boom then. There were a lot of shootings there. We lived in Queens first and people made fun of us for our Southern accent. The girls liked it but not the guys. People then thought people from the South were country bumpkins. Now it's cool to be from the South, but not then. We were living with my grandmother and uncle and mom was sending money while she went to school in Florida. I don't know where it went. Me and my brother looked like hobos but my grandmother had my sister looking like a princess. We were boys and girls are supposed to look pretty I guess. Me and my brother looked like a bunch of farmers." "What do you think about your sister getting stuff and you and your brother didn't?" I asked. Kevin just shrugged it off and said he didn't care, yet sharing the story with me during our interview showed he must have cared on some level.

He then told me about his mother taking him and his brother to her friend Jocelyn's house to visit for a weekend at Christmas. There he saw how other people lived. Jocelyn was a CEO with a huge house. They were welcomed in, had brunch, played with remote cars and had a great stay. Instead of being jealous, he realized that there was "something better out there" and he was going to find it both for himself and later, for his sons. His mother also remarried when he was ten, and his step-dad taught him about being a good father. "What I learned from him is that it's important to see a man get up in the morning and go to work. He worked every day in construction. He took me fishing and taught me how to work on cars. I still check on him now and I consider him my father."

Women Are to Blame for Men Being the Way They Are

"I have a lot of men friends and their women give them hell. And not just African American men; it's across the board."

Kevin loves to share his ideas and feelings about men and boys with friends and clients, and he often tells women that they are to blame for how men are today. "What do you mean?" I asked. "Well," he said, "I tell women, you get a boy and you coddle him, you keep him away from his father who can help him. There is a yin and yang between men and women. People wonder why boys are so emotional and things like this. First of all, they grow up in single mother households. I am not married to the moms of my kids now but I am very involved with my boys and have good relationships with their moms. There is not a day that goes by that I don't talk to my boys or see them.

"In my opinion, these days boys and girls are switching and girls are acting like boys and boys are acting more like girls because of the single parent home. This means that when you are a young boy and you see how your mom reacts when things go wrong by hollering and yelling, how do you think a boy is going to handle adversity? He is not going to handle it well. He is going to cry, shout and throw stuff.

"It is also hard when a man can't get access to his kids. My nephew is going through this situation right now. He has two kids and a good relationship with one of the moms but the other one has him in court right now. She is trying to get child support from him without him being allowed to be in the child's life. I keep telling women when they get mad that there are not enough 'masculine' men around, that 'you were that mother that had no expectations for your son so they end up on the couch playing video games. If the father of your child is worth any grain of salt, let him have a relationship with his child.'"

"Many women would tell you that the guy himself does not want a relationship with the kids," I said. "I don't think that is as true as what people say it is," said Kevin. "I have a lot of men friends and their women give them hell. And not just African American men, it's across the board. The women want to control what men do with the kids. I made sure I had 50/50 custody so I could do things like take them to sports games. My ex-wife knows I am a great dad and she doesn't try to stop me from taking them." But other men are not so lucky.

Men Are to Blame Too

It's not just women who are to blame, it's the men too and who they decide to have kids with, according to Kevin. "Men have to take the onus for the women they choose to lay down and have children with. I chose well with my son's moms. But there are a lot of red flags that men just ignore with the women they choose." "What are the red flags?" I asked. "All types of shit," he declared. "I talk to my older son [now seventeen] for example, so he can choose a girl. He is a great kid and he is at that age where he is talking to me about relationships and stuff. I tell him this stuff because I had to learn it on my own. It was through trial and error and asking myself tough questions.

Some men are just chicken-shit and afraid to look at what faults they have and are not willing to work on them."

"What are the faults men have?"

"Have you noticed how men choose the same type of woman? If you keep picking that same woman, this is where you need to talk to someone like you [a psychologist] or just ask themselves, 'why are the women I pick similar and all look the same? What is it?'

"In the black community, there is this thing about interracial relationships, and black women will say, 'you're with a white woman because she does everything you say.' But you have to look at the genesis of where people get their desires for different kinds of people. If my mom is always yelling at me at home and I go to school and Ms. Mary, the white lady teacher is nice to me, who do you think I will gravitate towards in my later dating life? Someone like my mom, or the woman who is nice to me? Often, men want a woman who speaks to them nicely. It's not about a white woman doing anything you say, it's about them being nice to men. People don't look at stuff like this. If you have a bad dynamic with your parent, you might be more attracted to someone who looks different but is nice. We choose people for a reason. I know white girls that will only date black men. Nine times out of ten, it has to do with something that has happened with a parent and it never fails. It's about vibe for me, that's what I like. But other people are different. The choices we make are from how we are brought up."

"What about the culture?" I asked. "The culture plays a part," said Kevin. "But it is hard to talk to men about how they grow up or become what they are. Women might get annoyed but will listen to my points, but men have a harder time. Men now take a feminine route because they are around a single mom and have not seen their dad properly handle conflict. My sons see that I handle things and don't throw stuff. When women get upset, they get mad, they'll bust up your car window. They'll key your car and holler. If a young boy sees that a lot, they are going to think that's the way things should be. I guarantee you if you take a kid from a single parent home versus a kid from a home with a father in it, the kid with the father in the home will be more emotionally aware. It is about time with dad."

Building Confidence

"What do you tell your sons that helps them be emotionally aware?" I asked. "I tell my sons to look people in the eye and give them a firm handshake when they meet someone," Kevin explained. "You're teaching them confidence," I added. "Yeah, that's right. Boys often don't learn confidence. Parents have to teach it. Look, kudos to my mom, she told me straight up that I needed to learn how to cook and clean so I don't need a woman. She also told me if you learn how to take care of yourself financially, you don't need someone to do that for you. My cousin, on the other hand, finds low confident men who she can buy a cell phone for or get them a car. Who the hell can't buy their own cell phone these days?

"If someone can easily get that stuff for you, they can easily take it away. These women are putting men in a position where they are needed by them and the men go along. You see that a lot these days, that men are dependent and willing to be that way. I tell my male friends, if you don't have any mail coming into your women's house, you're dependent, you're not a resident. You wonder why you are in this position? Well, I have a cousin who keeps having babies with this woman he clearly hates. He can't stand her! She is awful. He has a grown daughter from another relationship but with this awful woman, he's had twins, another kid and another kid. Why? He works eighteen hour shifts at a restaurant, then he comes home and cleans bottles and she doesn't work or do nothing. He calls me and complains."

"What about all the women who complain their husbands don't do enough?" I asked.

"All I ever hear from women is that they love their husband but are not in love with him. They all tell me that they married the man to get out of their house and have someone take care of them. I have come to realize that some women are selfish and using men to get out of certain situations, whether emotionally or physically." Kevin felt that men go along with this dependent setup, and when he brings it to their attention, they don't acknowledge the dynamic or try to change their behavior.

The Election, Spider Man, and Something Better

"Kamala ran a shit campaign…
she forgot that men vote too."

I interviewed Kevin right after the election so naturally wanted his view on the large numbers of men who voted for Trump versus those who voted for Harris. "About a quarter of black men and around 55 percent of men overall[91] voted for Trump.

---

[91] "Gender Gap: Voting Choices in Presidential Elections," Center for American Women and Politics, Eagleton Institute of Politics, Rutgers University. https://cawp.rutgers.edu/gender-gap-voting-choices-presidential-elections

What is your view on why men went so strongly for Trump this election?" I asked.

"Well, first of all, Kamala ran a shit campaign," he explained. "Everything was based off abortion and women's stuff and she forgot that men vote too. And it ended up with Obama and Michelle chastising black men[92] and I'm thinking 'why are *we* the target of why Kamala wasn't going to win.'

"This time, the Democratic Party has gone too far. It's into transgender stuff and not looking at what people were actually dealing with—eight or nine dollars for butter or eggs. Homelessness everywhere, mental health problems. I had a client ask me why I was voting for Trump. I'm the straight black dude everyone feels safe asking stuff—I guess I'm more objective. I think we have to be objective voters. I told her Trump would be beneficial for all people. But people always go back to why they don't like him as a person. I tell people to stop listening to sound bites and start looking at research on both sides and ask yourself 'who will I be better off with?' Black folks are basically conservative. We get trapped into other people's fights. The other groups are getting what they want under the Democrats and we're not, so what are we doing? Let's not be emotional about voting like I was for Obama the first time. Sure, I wanted to see a black man in there.

"But at the end of the day, my business was a lot more profitable under Trump. A female client got mad about me voting for Trump and said, 'Well what if one of your sons wanted to be a girl, wouldn't you assist in that?' I replied, 'if your child wanted to kill himself, would you assist him?' 'Well, no!' she

---

[92] Rashawn Ray and Keon L. Gilbert, "Why are Black men mad at Obama?" Brookings Institution, October 18, 2024. https://www.brookings.edu/articles/why-are-black-men-mad-at-obama/

said. 'Then why not get them some help so a young kid can figure out what they want to do. If they turn eighteen or twenty-
one and want to make that decision, God bless them. But if I
think I'm Spiderman at seven or eight, do you think my mom
was going to take me to the Empire State Building? No.' The
client seemed to get it when I put my concerns in common
language that she could relate to. She came to understand
another point of view. It's how the message is delivered that is
important. I try to present people with evidence or information
without getting overly emotional.

"I think this election has shown that people are sick of this
type of agenda that is pushed on us."

"What agenda is that?" I asked.

"That men ain't worth shit, this feminist movement. It's not
just men, it's the women too, I really believe that that is what
this election shows. There is so much bullshit now that people
are finally seeing it for what it is and are sick of it. Kamala
got blown out of the water. People want families. Women want
strong men, they want masculinity, but it goes back to the
problem which is that we [men] have the smaller microphone."
"Why is that?" I asked. "It's just the way it's designed," said
Kevin. "If we say anything as men, like you say, we get called
misogynistic. But it is our responsibility as men to have conversations and speak up. We need to keep our emotions out of it
and explain why we think how we do. As men, we need to keep
our emotions in check and express ourselves so people hear us."

Men Need a Microphone

"We have to write our own narrative."

"Men who speak up often get ostracized, fired, or thrown out of an organization," I said (James Damore, for example, who was fired from Google[93]). Kevin responded, "We, as men, need to get our own funding, do our own thing like grassroots stuff. Look, this is not 1908, there's ways to get things done. We have to write our own narrative. You can't let the powers that be and the public's opinion keep you down. When you have the right people and the right speakers in place, that stuff will be dispelled. Some men get ticked off and threaten or get emotional. As men, we need to conduct ourselves as men. We will get respect. We can't do what women do, I am not going to sit there and argue and do a bunch of tongue wrestling and screaming. I saw a guy jump out of his girlfriend's car at the gas station, screaming and crying, and I'm thinking like 'what the hell is wrong with you?' If a woman is getting you to the point where you are hitting stuff or screaming, you don't need them. It's time to go. It's the media who is trying to divide us up between men and women. It's up to us to go to women and say, 'I hear you and I want to understand you but I need you to hear me and understand me.' We need to look at things objectively. Respect how other people feel. But it has to go both ways. When you come at a woman with a mild calm tone, they will calm down. Don't just let it be with a woman and let it fester.

---

[93] Elizabeth Chuck, "James Damore, Google engineer fired for writing manifesto on women's 'neuroticism,' sues company," NBC News, January 8, 2018. https://www.nbcnews.com/news/us-news/google-engineer-fired-writing-manifesto-women-s-neuroticism-sues-company-n835836

"Look, at the end of the day, I just want something better for myself and my family." Now Kevin has an associate's degree in business management and a massage therapy license. He learned all he could about medical massage and healing, and now works with people post-surgery. He knew that traditional massage wouldn't pay the bills and found a niche market with women who needed recovery after liposuction or clients with back surgery that needed further post-op care. He proudly remarked that his business was thriving and his book is filled daily with clients. Before massage school, he had worked as a volunteer firefighter, at a factory and as an assistant manager. But he has found his place as an entrepreneur and business owner and spends his time helping people and feeling a sense of purpose. He came from sleeping on a mat in the NYC projects to owning a successful business in Tennessee. He has definitely found something better. But his success meant leaving the safety of working for a business to working for himself—taking a risk is sometimes the only way to get what you want.

In the next chapter, we will hear from men over fifty-five who have further thoughts and insights into life as a man in the current era. How did we get to the place where masculinity is viewed as a liability and female-centricity is dominating many aspects of men's lives? These older men have a bit more perspective than the younger ones and have sage advice for those younger men still in the trenches, especially when it comes to dating and marriage.

CHAPTER SIX

The Wisdom of Age:
Mature Men Speak Out

This chapter will discuss the interviews I conducted with men over fifty-five. These men have lived through drastic and unending cultural and legal changes that have impacted their dating and marital lives. These changes have taken place since they were very young. Their perspectives are much needed to help mentor younger men about these changes and hence, how to avoid the same problems. Although many of the older guys I interviewed were happy with their lives now, for some getting there was a difficult path—made harder by today's legal system and a culture that focuses on women's needs at the expense of men's.

But these men persevered and came out the other side even stronger (though some still had regrets). They became happier by finding a new life partner, finding peace in solitude, and by fulfilling their sense of purpose in the world. This sense of purpose is important throughout life, and it is one that gives men the strength to get through their day. Older men, in particular, are told that they serve little purpose in America. This is probably why the suicide rate in this age group is so high.

But this sense of purpose is necessary for happiness, according to researchers, especially as one gets older.[94] For men over fifty-five, there are different life tasks than in their earlier years. According to psychoanalyst Erik Erickson who analyzed the stages that people go through in life, these stages are referred to as "generativity vs. stagnation (middle adulthood)" and "integrity vs. despair (late adulthood)":

> *Stage 7—Generativity vs. stagnation (middle adulthood): Adults think about their contributions to society, seek to make a positive impact, and find fulfillment through productive work and nurturing relationships.*

> *Stage 8—Integrity vs. despair (late adulthood): Older adults reflect on their lives and find a sense of satisfaction or regret.*[95]

It is hard to contribute to society when the society itself says that men are not valued—but the men I interviewed had found a way of life that worked for them, on their own terms. Their lives aren't perfect but they are surviving and thriving

---

[94] Renée Onque, "This is what the happiest people 'get right' at an early age, says director of Harvard's 86-year happiness study," CNBC, December 20, 2024. https://www.cnbc.com/2024/12/20/happiness-expert-what-the-happiest-people-get-right-at-an-early-age.html

[95] Sarah Jividen, "Generativity vs. Stagnation in Middle Adulthood," Very Well Health, updated April 17, 2025. https://www.verywellhealth.com/generativity-vs-stagnation-7550473

despite the trend that sees older men as liabilities rather than survivors to be treated with respect.

Randy

"These women were bottomless pits of need."

"I like myself and I'm not changing who I am and what I value in order to be married."

My first interview in this age group was with Randy, a fifty-seven-year-old black military veteran; he is tall and works as a personal trainer. Randy has been married three times and still retains his sense of humor and positive outlook on life and people, so I thought he would be a great interview, which turned out to be correct. He was initially reticent, but later texted me that an interview would be fine. We ended up discussing his life and feelings over several interviews and he was forthcoming with the details of his life and marriages and why they didn't work for him.

We met up for the first interview at his work and he told me that he was born in Chattanooga, Tennessee. His early life was fairly stable though his parents divorced when he was young. He had an older brother and later a younger brother. His mother took him and his brother to live in Knoxville, and his dad stayed in Chattanooga.

Randy admits that he was puzzled as to why his dad never saw them much even though he only lived two hours away. "My dad was not involved in our lives." He would see him occasionally but spent most of his time with his mother and older brother. "My older brother was only eleven months older than me. We were almost like twins because we were in the same grade. He picked fights with me because I never struggled with much; life was easy for me and came naturally. Like school, I just did it and he struggled." Randy did not particularly like school, he just felt like "he had to do it" so why get upset?

He described his mother as very "hands on," which meant she "kept us out of trouble and always grounded me if I went near anyone who was trouble." His mother remarried and had another son, and Randy felt his stepfather was a good man and the marriage was a good one for his mother. Randy appreciated her care very much but wanted to start his own life and joined the army at seventeen. He wanted freedom from his mother telling him what to do and wanted to make more of his own decisions in the wider world.

Marriage Number One

In the military, he worked in an artillery unit and later worked in refueling and as an accounting officer, and spent a good deal of time traveling around the US and Korea. The work was easy for him though he did admit that it was not all that challenging. He met his first wife, "Angel," when he was around twenty in Colorado Springs at a night club for enlisted men. She was not in the Army, though her father was an officer and civilians were allowed to go to the night clubs, and it was a good place for women and enlisted men to meet. Randy says their attraction was instant and they married soon after they met.

Their marriage initially was good and they travelled often but "then it got really bad." His wife was using drugs and alcohol, which he denied having knowledge of before they were married. "She drank and stuff but it didn't seem like an issue. I think the drugs changed her." Once he found out she was using, he tried to help her but she didn't want to cooperate. He learned that she was using their credit cards around the base to go on spending sprees. When his checks were not enough to cover her bills, the base quit accepting their credit card. He stated that he had to sign papers that she could no longer use the credit card in order to stop the constant cash outflow.

Despite the problems, the couple stayed married for around fourteen years and had two daughters. Eventually, when the children were eight and ten, his wife took them and went to California because her parents lived there. Randy explained that his base continued to send dependent pay to his wife. It was hard to get a divorce because he had to go to Korea and could not make it back to court. A judge in California did not grant the divorce because his wife said she didn't want one. And why would she, with child support and dependent care funds being sent to her through Randy's military job? Randy stated that she kept the money that was being sent for his children. His divorce finally came through, and he continued to pay for child support.

Finally, when he got back to the US, the state of California said he was in arrears on child support, and Randy took matters into his own hands. "I got permission to go see about my kids, got in my car and drove to California. I had records of all the money I had sent and checks that I wrote. I had the evidence and I wanted to secure legal guardianship of the kids." He did not get custody at that time, even though his wife was using drugs and her parents had the kids for the most part.

I asked him if it bothered him that the state of California came after him, even though he was making the child support payments. He said, "No, I went to prove to my kids that I was involved and that I cared." He wanted his kids to know he was not like his "uninvolved dad." He did not seem to blame the "system" or have had ill-will; it was "just the way it is." This was a common theme with the men I interviewed who encountered discrimination or legal repercussions for the simple act of being male. They did not typically complain, but saw it as "just the way the system is." It was not a passive conclusion, it seemed to be a choice not to focus on what could not be fixed, but what could. I admired Randy's fortitude, but wondered if men were so used to being under scrutiny by the legal system that they just figured it wasn't worth the fight, or it was just like the weather—brewing in the background and just something to put up with.

Finally, in 2001, Randy got custody of his two daughters and a divorce only through "luck." His ex had a drug-addicted baby by another man and the kids went into state custody. One day, Randy got a call from the Red Cross, who asked him if he was willing or able to take the kids. He went back to California, got a lawyer and was able to get full custody of the kids and a divorce, as the ex-wife never showed up to court. He was stationed in Germany and his kids were eleven and thirteen, and went to live with his mother in Tennessee until he finished his military service.

Marriage Number Two

During his time in Germany, he met his second wife, Ava, who he described as "young and emotionally immature." She was also in the military and "I loved her.... All my relationships start out stable and at some point, another side of them comes out." His second wife was controlling. For example, when she was stationed in Korea in a different time zone, she would call Randy at two in the morning, drinking and asking him why he didn't say much. "I was asleep" was not a good enough answer if he didn't immediately take her call. Or she would get mad and demanding, "Where were you?" She would act as if he were out partying or running around when he was home trying to sleep. This behavior concerned him, but he wanted Ava to live with him and be a family with his two daughters.

He wanted to get stationed at Fort Campbell, Kentucky to be closer to his daughters and she agreed. However, after talking to her twin sister who was in the Air Force, she changed her mind and said she did not want to move and wanted a divorce. She threatened divorce when she did not get her way and Randy finally just told her, "Give me the papers and I will sign them." He retired from the military at thirty-seven and went back to Tennessee to be with his kids.

Marriage Number Three

Around 2005, he was working as a personal trainer which was his passion. "I love helping people," he stated. At one point, he gave a demonstration training session to a woman, Jesse, who left and came back a few months later to start training with him. She had gotten divorced in the interim, and Randy started dating her after a period of time. Two years later, they got married and initially, everything seemed fine. She had a couple of kids as well, and Randy stated that he "treated her kids as if they were mine." He cleaned, cooked, and helped with whatever was needed in the house. He says he didn't think much about it at first. "That's what you do when you are married."

As time went on, he realized that she was controlling, but then it got worse. She was a realtor who made a good living and would use it to try and control Randy. "She would question me if I got twenty dollars out of an ATM. That was the first tip something was wrong." She would tell him that she earned the money, even though he was working and had a military pension. One day she told him to get pizza for her kids and he thought she meant for dinner. When the pizza when not delivered by 3:30 or 4pm, she let him have it, and chastised him in front of the kids. "She did not respect me and treated me like I was one of her kids." His wife was also upset that he did not share her interests. Randy gave an example of a time when she asked him to go skiing. When he said no, he wasn't a skier, she got even angrier.

"She spent a lot of time on social media and there was always some drama going on there that I did not have time for. She was always trying to tell me about what was happening online and was even accusing me of getting on to look at other women. Once she even accused me of having an affair with our housekeeper who was an old friend. I was like 'what the heck?'"

"Money was a constant issue. She even questioned me when I tried to help my mother get her floors repaired. It was like a couple hundred bucks. She asked me if we were going to be supporting my mom forever. Meanwhile, she paid any amount for her parents to travel and do other things."

The final straw came when she threatened to divorce him if he didn't vote Republican. "I told her I'm a black man in America and am not voting Republican. Then she got online to ask her friends if it was okay to stay married to someone with different political views. I was like 'hello, why don't you talk to me, your husband instead of some people on the internet?'" Randy's experience of being pushed to vote the way his wife did is not that unusual. Despite a 2024 pro-Harris ad insinuating that men push women into voting *their* way,[96] just the opposite is true. Men were four points more likely than women to report feeling too much pressure from their spouse to vote a certain way according to *Echelon Insights*.[97] Randy and his wife divorced some time after this incident and Randy has been single for the past five or six years.

Peace at Last

"I am who I am and no one is going to change me. That's not how it works. These women always want to change men. They are looking for a perfect man and that doesn't exist." Randy says it's been a long road but, "I am at peace. I don't have to change myself for anyone. I make myself happy. Why should I build a woman up? Who is going to build me up?"

These days, Randy enjoys training his clients and spending time with his daughters and grandson. He has a "female friend" currently but has no plans of marrying again. He stays off the internet and social media and says they are negative energy. "I have always been a positive guy and I don't need negative energy in my life. I have no time for negative people or the drama that comes from social media. Women are all into that and I don't have the time."

Finally, at the end of our series of interviews, I asked Randy how he would describe being a man in today's America. "I can't answer that," he stated. "I live in my own bubble and don't look

---

[96]   Soleil Ho, "A pro-Harris ad reminds women that their votes are secret— and right-wing media is furious," *San Francisco Chronicle*, November 4, 2024. https://www.sfchronicle.com/opinion/soleilho/article/pro-harris-ad-reminds-women-votes-secret-19880418.php

[97]   Echelon Insights (@EchelonInsights), "When asked about where this pressure came from...," X, December 6, 2024. https://x.com/EchelonInsights/status/1865065399621992818

to the left or right. I have my own positive energy and look for the positive in life. I don't get out there in the drama. I am finally at peace."

Notice the difference between how Randy handled his second and third marriages and his first. When kids are involved, it makes it harder for men both legally and psychologically to get out of a marriage, even if it is abusive or simply utilitarian as a way to get funding for a woman's needs. Because Randy had high regard for himself and his well-being, he was able to call their bluff when his second and third wives wanted a divorce. "Okay, just give me the papers" is not typically expected in today's entitled culture.

If Charlie in the last chapter had simply filed for divorce early, it might have made the difference in his moving beyond an abusive situation quickly. But he was used to an addictive mother and couldn't bring himself to reject his first wife. Charlie's situation was unlike Randy's, who had a good relationship with his mother and high self-regard so he was less likely to allow himself to be a hostage to his emotions. The psychology of men plays a part in keeping them in a bad marriage, just like women. They are human but no one gives a man that benefit. Because men usually have to figure things out for themselves, it is good to be an astute observer of human nature and to protect yourself if you feel that your wife or girlfriend does not have your best interests at heart. That does not necessarily mean a divorce or breakup, but it means that if you see behavior that leaves you feeling upset, angry, hurt, or anything similar, make a note of it. Then if it becomes a pattern, decide early if this is the right woman for you before it is too late.

Several of the men I interviewed felt that men did not always look after their best interests or they kept chasing the same type of toxic woman. Others like Wyatt, the next interviewee, understood too well that the wrong woman was not an option. But finding the right one has still been elusive for him.

Wyatt

"Feminism is about what is convenient for her."

"One bad date asked me if I was a misogynist."

Wyatt is a native-born San Franciscan but his family is Norwegian in origin. He is fifty-six, an engineer, lives in the Bay Area and has been there most of his life. We talked over a seventy-five-minute Zoom call and what I remember most from our interview was that Wyatt's dad committed suicide when he was just seven years old. "From that day on, I put my toys away and kept my room clean so mom wouldn't leave me too. I learned that I was afraid of being abandoned from a therapist when I was twenty-five." Wyatt seemed to have everything going for him except for a relationship, and for a long time he blamed himself. He told me during the interview that "I started reading a lot of books from you, Jordan Peterson and others who talk about men and I learned I wasn't the sole cause of the problem."

Dating in a Blue State

I asked him to describe the Bay Area dating scene, as many of my previous interviewees had been from the South and it is different culturally in many ways. Wyatt responded, "It's not good and it is even worse than when I was younger. If you are a white, heterosexual guy, it's real difficult. You are guilty until proven innocent."

"What about other parts of the country, did you find them different in terms of relationships and people?" I asked. "Yes, I've been to Tennessee a few times for music festivals. I have been to Kentucky and I go to Florida for scuba diving. I notice that I mostly visit the red states where men are men and women are women. Dating is undoubtedly different in the red states. Here in San Francisco, the women have pink hair, nipple rings, hair like it was cut in a wind storm and tattoos up to their neck. I am pretty acceptable on whatever, but when it comes to dating, I've got my preferences so…I have no problem with same sex marriage because I don't have the right to tell other people what to do. But at the same time, I have my own preferences, too, and if you don't meet them, I would rather stay single." "Do women ask you about your preferences?" I asked. "Well, the last date I went on, she asked me if I was a misogynist (someone who hates women). It was an odd question to ask. They're just a different animal here. It is ground zero for feminists here." "How did you meet this woman?" I asked. "I worked with her. She is very overweight and I just wanted to go out and have a good time, have some fun. I asked her why she asked me that question and she said, 'No reason, I just wanted to ask.' I haven't seen her since the date."

Wanting to know more about Wyatt's earlier dating experience, I asked if dating was different when he was young and he described himself as a "late bloomer." "In high school, I was there in the 80s, it wasn't so radically feminist then, but I really didn't start dating until college. I was in a rock band, never really had a girlfriend and just hooked up with people a lot. I asked one person to marry me once that I had known since second grade. I ran into her in college again and she wanted to get married after college but I didn't so she married someone else. Fast forward ten years later, she saw me on Facebook and she had just divorced and got in touch. I was kind of living in nostalgia—we went to Montessori school together—and I asked her to marry me but she said no. She got breast cancer and there was a lot of drama but she is in remission now. We are still friends."

"Have you tried the dating apps?" I asked. "Oh, God, yes. I don't like any of them. I tried Match, Bumble, Plenty of Fish…. There are not a lot of attractive single women in the Bay Area. Everyone thinks that, this being California, all the women are good-looking here but maybe in LA. Most here in the Bay are overweight, dress like guys, and just not feminine. I don't have much of a dating pool here. The women here want a tall guy. I am six [foot] three, I make good money, have a second job. I like to scuba dive, dive with sharks. I'm in a band. I have a lot going for me so I'm going to look for someone with a lot going for her too. She doesn't have to have the same interests, just keep herself in shape, be feminine and those two things alone is like I'm asking for the world."

Superficial and Looking for Status

Some of Wyatt's friends think he should write a book about all of his dating experiences, given the types of behaviors he has encountered on various dates. "There is a lot of superficiality. If you take Marin County which is across the bridge, San Mateo, and San Francisco, we have one of the most affluent places in the United States. There is a lot of money here and San Francisco is a very transient city, so many people are from different areas and parts of the country. A lot of women come here and are looking for dates and guys with a lot of money. It is very superficial. Most are from the US. I have had women ask me on the first date 'what's your 401k look like?'

"I now just weed through conversations for the first hour with a date to see if they are just superficial and looking for money. I know now how to ask the right questions." "What are the right questions?" I asked. "I just look for things in general for a tip-off that one date is all. One woman wouldn't get in my car. I met her at a bar at a friend's party. We were going to go to another party and she saw my car; it wasn't nice enough and I had to wave her down a taxi and meet her at the party. She later said, 'I thought you had a Jaguar or something.' I have a nice pickup truck but it wasn't good enough, even though I told her I would get her there safely. Another yoga teacher I met was nice. I invited her to my house to give her a houseplant as a gift, and all she did is ask me how much everything in my house cost."

"Are there any women there who you have met who aren't superficial?" I asked. "Not really, for me anyway. I was even part of a dating agency where I paid $3000 to get twenty-four dates a year. Each date got more and more overweight and overbearing. It is just not good. I think it is not just here. I think the relationships between men and women here in America are just not healthy."

Views on Marriage

"Even my friends who are married, half of them are divorced. Most of those have gone through nasty divorces—one friend had a wife where she says she won't touch his 401k and then she takes half as soon as she could prior to the divorce. I have two other friends who have daughters. Both their wives decided they didn't want to be mothers anymore and left. So the stereotype of how men are always the one trying to leave the relationship because they are scared of commitment? That wasn't the case with my friends." Wyatt stopped at that point in the interview and said, "I don't want you to think I hate women." "Why would I think that?" I asked.

It seems that legitimate concerns about relationships with women cause men to feel that they are doing something wrong if they speak up. *If women complain about men nonstop, it's normal. If men even have a concern, they are misogynists.* It is a difficult psychological place to be when you are a man just looking for some human comfort and connection.

Wyatt confirmed this latter point when he told me it was rare to talk about this "stuff" with anybody, much less a woman, and it was refreshing. "It is hard for a man to be open about how he really feels about life and women. If I even tell a woman I want someone feminine, I am called a misogynist." Wyatt has regrets about how his love life has gone. "I'm old enough now to be past disappointed. Do I feel a void, like did I wish I could have found a girlfriend or wife? Yes, I think I would have made a good father."

Red Pilled

"What made you quit dating?" I asked.

"Three or four years ago, I quit dating. I read you, Rollo Tomassi, Jordan Peterson and others and it resonated with me. I started reading more about female nature and about how hypergamy (women wanting higher status men to date or marry) works. I realized it wasn't just me, I'm not the sole problem. It helped me understand why I am still single and it has been helpful. There are more and more single guys out there every day. Men are finding other things to do than look for women." "Are they happier finding other things to do?" I asked. "Yes, I do think they are. And I feel like I am past the point of no return in that regard, but younger guys should have a chance to find a relationship. Maybe if they change some of the laws that are unfavorable to men, like you wrote about in your last book. But for me, the older I get, the more I have to lose than I did twenty years ago. It is harder to trust women now. I have been on a lot of dates that have reinforced that."

Work and DEI

We talked a little about his job as an engineer. He works for a large utility company in Silicon Valley and has been there over twenty years. He likes his job a lot and feels that he helps people with his work. He has on-the-job training and feels a great deal of competence at work.

I asked him about DEI (diversity, equity and inclusion) at his company and if it affected him. He responded, "Oh yes, this is San Francisco, my company has DEI big time. It hasn't affected me, because I am just used to it. The last two CEOs were women and the current woman who is CEO I like a lot. Both of the African American men that were hired as vice presidents left as soon as they got their bonus. I am just used to being a white male at work. I think where I live a lot of guys just give up on the notion of ever moving up the ladder, just like they feel about never finding a woman. There is just a deep-seated acceptance that you have to deal with, that most of the higher-ups are going to be people of color or women. As long as they are the best person for the job, I have no problem with that. But if you are just hiring them because they are the right color or sex, I don't agree with that. You should hire the best person for the job."

"Do you think men accept a lot of what happens to them without standing up for themselves?" I asked. I was thinking about Randy in the last section who just accepted that the state of California came after him for child support, even though he was paying it. And here was Wyatt, saying essentially the same thing—that men just accept what the system does to them. "Well, I think the acceptance from men comes because of the laws. They are a huge mountain that we would have to climb or a task too big to take on and so we just go with it. Men also have a tendency to not complain and just take our lumps."

Depression and Anxiety

"Depriving a child of his or her dad is like depriving a child part of her or his life." [98]

I wondered at this point in our conversation if men had repercussions emotionally for just accepting what is dished out or "just taking their lumps," and mentioned to Wyatt the high rate of suicide among men. "What about men's psyche?" I asked him. "How do you think men process this discriminatory treatment?" Wyatt paused at this point and said, "This ties into my childhood. I didn't have the best one." At this point, Wyatt's voice became weary and he continued.

"I lost my dad at seven…he committed suicide. So it was an uphill battle for my brother and I. I had a younger brother who was four and I had to grow up real quick after that. When I took my psychology classes in college, I learned that as a boy losing your father figure, it was the exact most impressionable age for me. I got hit pretty hard with it. My brother didn't get hit as hard because he didn't have the time to make as big an

---

[98]   Farrell and Gray, *The Boy Crisis*. 105.

attachment. I got gut punched hard. It took me years to get off my knees.

"My mom kind of brushed it under the rug, I love her, she is a strong woman and she had to take care of two kids when my dad died. She didn't want to talk about it. I don't really know the whole story as to why he killed himself. Sometimes all it takes is for a woman to say, 'you know what, you're acting crazy, I'm taking the kids away.' That's all it takes and the guy is done. I don't know if that's what happened but later on, my friend's mom who had a PhD in psychology saw me in my mid-twenties. She was shocked that I hadn't talked to anyone about my dad. What doesn't kill you makes you stronger. Unlike my dad, I've never been suicidal but I've got some anxiety. I would rather fight it out than take myself out."

As Wyatt was talking, it made sense to me that he didn't trust women. He was afraid of being abandoned by his mom and in a deep way, she hurt him by never talking about his father or his feelings. Later, she remarried and his mother told him to start calling the new man "dad." He must have felt that his dad's life was not very important to her, as if his dad had been nonexistent. Men's lives are often expendable to society and to women; male children pick up on this and internalize other people's lack of empathy for them as just part of being a man.

Now the "empowered women" in the Bay Area, like Wyatt's mom, don't want to hear what men think or feel—maybe because they are afraid, maybe for fear of blame, or maybe just due to a narcissism that doesn't allow them to see outside themselves. Or it gives them a feeling of power to put down a man and their peers back them up. It is troubling to say the least.

Wyatt summed up his feelings as we talked. "I don't want anyone to feel sorry for me. Financially and spiritually, I feel that I am doing really well, maybe *because* I had to deal with so much. I think much of the difficulty finding a relationship now is that I am traditional in my outlook and the women here are progressive."

Women and Politics

Wyatt brings up a good point, which is that many of the differences today between men and women have to do with the contrast of men's more right-leaning political leanings and the progressive programming of today's women. It makes empathy (a necessary component for a relationship) for men harder and creates a gap between the sexes that leaves many people out in the cold. And women are much less willing to date a man who is right-leaning.[99]

Pew Research did a survey on dating, asking single people what would keep them from dating a potential mate. It turns out politics is a real factor: "Among Democrats and those who lean toward the Democratic Party who are single but looking for a relationship, about seven-in-ten (71%) say they probably or definitely would not consider being in a committed relationship with someone who voted for Donald Trump. In fact, 45% say they *definitely* would not consider seriously dating a Trump voter."[100] And it is easy to see why opposites don't attract when looking at the large chasm between men and women's views. A

---

[99] Alejandra O'Connell-Domenech, "Politics are increasingly a dating dealbreaker—especially for women," *The Hill*, March 25, 2023. https://thehill.com/changing-america/enrichment/arts-culture/3917348-politics-are-increasingly-a-dating-dealbreaker-especially-for-women/

[100] Anna Brown, "Most Democrats who are looking for a relationship would not consider dating a Trump voter," Pew Research Center, April 24, 2020. https://www.pewresearch.org/short-reads/2020/04/24/most-democrats-who-are-looking-for-a-relationship-would-not-consider-dating-a-trump-voter/

Wall Street Journal article called "America's New Political War Pits Young Men Against Young Women" had charts highlighting the differences in political leanings between the sexes.

Women are more likely to see an urgency to address climate change, forgive student loans, support abortion, don't want the Trump tax cuts extended, and are more likely than men to allow children to choose gender identity without parental approval. Knowing that most women they date lean left gives men pause to share their views. "Some men interviewed said they were fearful of criticism by women and expressed their resentments only in private and with other men. Several said they hide their conservative views because women they know have said they won't date right-leaning men."[101] With so little trust, how can you have a meaningful relationship?

I get why a man dating a woman casually might not share his political views but if the relationship turns more serious, wouldn't it be better to find out how a prospective long-term partner will treat you? If she opposes your views *and* doesn't respect you, that seems like a red flag, one which too many men ignore to their peril. One who didn't is the next interviewee who found a woman who respected him and his political views.

Jack, is a seventy-year-old libertarian who finally found a woman that is compatible with him both politically and emotionally. But it was a long road. He has good advice for younger men navigating today's dating market—it's best to find an outlier like he did. Jack's interview and the next one are a little different. Rather than ask a lot about their background,

---

[101] Aaron Zitner and Andrew Restuccia, "America's New Political War Pits Young Men Against Young Women," *The Wall Street Journal,* July 28, 2024. https://www.wsj.com/politics/policy/men-women-vote-republican-democrat-election-7f5f726c?st=sttnjmrpzlpkhpa&reflink=article_imessage_share

I asked more about their opinions on how the treatment of men has changed over the years as well as for their advice for younger men. They are both very successful and older and have much to teach other men about finding a good woman who is loving and cares about them, even after being divorced more than once. They also had much to say about life and work and how the PC culture makes it harder for men, even successful ones like themselves.

One thing here I want to point out is that in our society, we are told that older people have nothing to teach young ones, that their experiences are dated and irrelevant. This is done on purpose by the liberal media and elites who want young guys under their thumb or that of a woman, or, if single, miserable rather than happy and independent. In the past, young men learned from older ones, often dads and grandfathers. But with more fatherless kids now, it is harder to interact with older men who have tons of experience and knowledge about being a man. Listen to their experiences in the following sections and decide if they have something to teach you about women and the world.

Jack

"Find an outlier if you want to be happy."

"With age, women aren't as entitled."

Jack was a science reporter when he was younger. He is now a writer who lives in Manhattan and shares an apartment there part-time with his new wife, Joan. He keeps another place further out of the city in Westchester to give himself some breathing room and some alone time. His new wife agrees with this arrangement, saying that it is best for their marriage. How did he find someone who fits into his lifestyle and allows him to be himself? And more importantly, how did he find a woman who genuinely likes and appreciates men in NYC? We talked for an hour and a half by Zoom so I could find out how he got so lucky.

Jack stated he got married during COVID in 2020 out in Wyoming without masks. This is his third marriage. The first one lasted three years; the second, twenty years (they have one child, a son) and he has now been married for the third time for over four years. His first two wives had substance abuse problems, particularly his son's mother. One day around 2012, after his mother's fourth stint in rehab, his son, Liam, said to Jack, "Dad, don't stick around for me." They left the house and went to live on their own and life got better for them. A couple of years ago, his second wife died, Jack said sadly. "On a more positive note, I call my new wife, 'The Great Outlier.' She is not really a feminist. We never argue. I just can't believe marriage could be this great." "How did you meet such a gem?" I asked.

"I met her in NYC. After me and my last wife split up, I went to a party in 2014 at a mutual friend's apartment where I met Joan. She is very academic and smart, and I was impressed. We started seeing each other after the party but I told her 'I never want to get married again. I never want to be in a serious relationship again.'"

"Why do you think it worked out with her then?" I asked. "I think it has to do with age. [His new wife is near to his age.] The younger women today have been fed so much feminist stuff and they are so entitled. It is so toxic for relationships, I don't have to tell you, but women who grew up on this diet of 'we're better than men and the only reason we aren't running this country is they're holding us back' is bad for relationships."

Fairness and Hormones

"My wife is very fair and not a feminist. She is very empathetic and very feminine in some ways."

"Do men like feminine women?" I asked, thinking of my last interviewee, Wyatt, who was berated for wanting a date to be feminine. "Oh, yeah, of course." stated Jack. I told Jack about Wyatt's issues with his dates calling him a misogynist and asked him for advice for younger men on how to find an outlier like he did.

"I would look for a woman who is fair and empathetic to men," Jack stated. This of course, is easier said than done. How do you know if a woman is fair-minded and empathetic? Jack mentioned that an acute sense of justice and fairness are traits linked with the testosterone system in the brain. This does seem to be the case. One study I read stated that even *women* given testosterone were less aggressive and more fair.[102]

The stereotype is that testosterone makes men more competitive and willing to cut corners and take advantage to get ahead. But actually, it's the reverse, and even in women. When women get testosterone without knowing it, they become more

---

[102] "Testosterone leads to fairness, not aggression: researchers," CBC News, December 8, 2009. https://www.cbc.ca/news/science/testosterone-leads-to-fairness-not-aggression-researchers-1.796578

cooperative and more concerned with fairness. But when they THINK they're getting it and don't, they become more aggressive and willing to cheat. This kind of fits the stereotype—masculine men are thought to be bluff and honest, unmasculine men are stereotyped as conniving—for example the weasel character in a movie tends to be a small, unmasculine man.

So while men might want a feminine woman, they should also remember that a very feminine woman is more likely to have a princess personality. If you have tried dating women who turn out to be entitled or what you perceive to be less giving and more likely to think men are there to serve them, maybe give the tomboys a chance. If they have more testosterone, they may be more likely to be fair or at least more likely to empathize with men. (Note, these are my words, not Jack's here.) Or at the very least, according to this *Medium* article, "Tomboys are approachable and down-to-earth, making them great companions. Men appreciate the lack of pretense and the genuine nature of tomboys. This quality fosters a comfortable and authentic connection that is often sought after in relationships."[103]

But let's get back to Jack and hear his views on women and complaining, something that has always been common but is now more prevalent given the increase in the world of Karens, particularly since the COVID pandemic.

---

[103] Stanley Parker, "Unveiling the Allure: Why are Tomboys so attractive to Men?" *Medium*, January 31, 2024. https://blueheartbeat.medium.com/why-are-tomboys-so-attractive-4165c8916451

The Complaint Gap

"Women get power by complaining."

Jack continued our discussion about women and how complaining works in their favor. "When women show weakness and are seen as victims, they get sympathy and help, and men don't. People don't like seeing men weak—neither sex likes it. Woman say they want a sensitive man but they really don't. Instead, women really want the strong silent type because what is the alternative, the weak chatty type? By complaining, women achieve what they want and men don't. Women get power by complaining. I do think guys are freer to talk about things now which is a good thing. I went to therapy and it did help me, though I do wish I could get my money back sometimes. But, this is where guys gain, they can talk more freely about their feelings now."

"Sure, maybe men can talk to a therapist if they are good and egalitarian, but what about talking to other people in society?" I asked.

"Well, I can see why guys just retreat to the manosphere[104] because you just don't say what you really think—you will be branded a misogynist. My son is a conservative and libertarian. It's hard because he went to such a woke high school. When Trump won the election in 2016, the whole school was in mourning. He just kept his mouth shut because what else do you do?" "So where do young men go to be heard," I asked.

---

[104] The manosphere is a collection of websites and places online that men can go to talk to each other about women or misandry, the hatred of men. I tried to find a decent online definition to link to but most of the sources were negative —stating that any man visiting these sites is toxic, angry, and probably violent. Note that it is so threatening for men to have a place to voice their real feelings that everyone wants to shut them down.

Where Do Men Go?

"I think young men now turn to guys like Jordan Peterson[105] [the psychologist mentioned earlier who writes and talks with men about their issues]. There is a good market for that, and young guys are eager to find things that jibe with reality that you don't find in the mainstream media. And even on places like social media and Facebook, you are afraid to put anything down because you will be cancelled. Today, all the characters in movies are like one-hundred-pound women beating up men and it is so unrealistic. I think young guys now have it hard. If a guy, like my son, is conservative, and he and his friends are really leery of left-wing girls. But there are a lot of liberal girls, right? Like over 50 percent of them. And it is a bad strategy for the women since it limits their dating pool. It is great strategy for feminist activists since they get a lot of single women who are looking for an outlet for their anger and want the government to grow and support them. Women have always been in favor of bigger government, they know where the money is coming from." This bigger government theme has been mentioned by other men and is one area where men are willing to go against women, probably due to the anonymity of the voting booth. There will be overall anger towards men for voting against large government but fewer consequences for any individual man.

Double Standards

As Jack talked, I thought about how women can be angry with men and it is seen as empowerment. The culture, academia, and the media tell women that they are justified to show hostility

---

[105] See https://www.jordanbpeterson.com/

towards men. However, if men are angry and look online or express their feelings, they are treated as toxic, dangerous and possibly violent.

"What do you do if you are a man who is frustrated with his situation?" I asked him.

"Hmm, I guess try not to write off all women from what you hear in messages from the mainstream media about what women want or what they are like. I do know liberal women who take in a lot of what they hear from these messages but at the same time, these same women want to be treated like a woman. They like the door opened for them, they like to feel protected. For guys, try to find someone out there who is not caught up in the stereotypes and accepts reality."

At this point I said to Jack, "Yes, these 'feminist' women want someone to open the door, and pay for things, but at the same time, there is a double standard. If these women are making any money, they will see it as theirs. They expect the man to pay and open doors while they espouse their feminist views. I interviewed one man (Randy) who couldn't even take twenty bucks out of the ATM because his 'feminist wife' told him she made the money and he wasn't to spend even his *own* money. This is very common—the double standards. Men will often put up with it if they are married."

"Don't get me wrong," Jack stated. "It took me years to get out of my second divorce—too long, so I get it."

The double standards are real, not only in the world of relationships but in the world of work. Jack told me about his experiences as a white heterosexual man in the media business and stated, "I was always a writer and never really wanted to be an editor or anything so it didn't matter much to me. But at the newspaper I worked at, I think at one point they called in all the middle-aged white guys and said, 'look, you're not going to rise any higher.' So one editor who I knew looked elsewhere."

"What do you think men feel when they hear these negative messages against them from either their wives or girlfriends or at work? Or at school. I talked with guys who say they feel bad when they are blamed for all the ills of the world while they are in a classroom." Jack reflected on this and said, "I guess they feel disrespected and unappreciated. My new wife is so appreciative and always thanks me for taking out the garbage or helping with things around the house.

"I guess I would tell guys it's not our fault, and that men have done so much for mass culture. Men have created the culture and women are pissed off and are trying to tell us that it is *us* who is stopping them from doing the same; and it is remarkable that in fifty years of feminism how little they have done. For example, women's sports have come a long way but they don't *invent* sports.

"Evolution is such that women choose men who can be manipulated. Men are stronger physically and are better at doing some of the big group tasks. Women are more sophisticated emotionally and are better at manipulating men, and they select men who will go out and work all day and turn over the proceeds to their wives. Once sex became more available outside of marriage, all this changed, I guess. For example, there was a survey I read where men were asked, 'how would you feel if a woman had sex with a robot,' and the men answered 'fine.' The women, however, really felt threatened if men did the same. That is taking away their trump card. Women gave away their trump card when they gave away sex without commitment." We then discussed how hard it is to find an outlier, a woman who likes men and isn't out to feel threatened or as if a man is just there as a meal ticket and punching bag.

"When I was dating between marriages, I heard all these cliches about how men want younger women and I was like, 'who wants these women raised on this nonsense?' What advice would I tell guys on how to find an outlier? There aren't enough women around who are like that, and of course women have the other problem in that there aren't enough guys around who are higher status. There is this huge mismatch."

I pointed out the irony that women are asking for numerous outlying expectations such as height, high status, high income, and things of that nature, while all a man is asking for is that he not be treated badly. Jack laughed and said, "yes, the whole six-six-six rule" [a man needs to be six feet tall, make a six figure income, and have six pack abs—or in some versions, at least a six-inch penis]. We turned to talking about how the dating apps had raised expectations and that the men were not viewed as "good enough." "Yes, women swipe left three times as often as men is what I have heard," Jack stated. Their politics also play a part and toward the end of the interview, Jack said, "I guess what I would say is that both of my wives from my first two marriages were liberal—not crazy liberals but who knows about the politics...not sure how that affected us." I would say it was a factor.

Thoughts on School

I asked Jack at the end of the interview if there was anything more he would like to add to help boys and men and he turned to how much his school years affected him as a guy. "Yes, I also want to say that I went to an all-boys school in Chile and it was just perfect."

"What made it perfect?"

"We had uniforms and then when we got to school, we put on overalls so we didn't have to worry about getting dirty. You would run around and play soccer after every class. We had a lot of male teachers. Every class had rankings of who was doing best in the class and boys loved this stuff. At the end of the year in third grade, there was this giant awards ceremony where you put on a parade uniform and got medals and things. It really was what it took to motivate boys. And then, I come back [to the US] and I went to a coed school from around fourth to eighth grade and it was completely different. There was a lot of social anxiety. It was about what you wore, you couldn't run on the playground, you sat in these chairs all day, and the girls were all about cliques.

"Then I went back to a Catholic all-boys high school and there were no cliquish groups. Sure, there were different groups who sat in the lunch room, but we had a different social life and it was much easier. The teachers taught, and in the school newspaper there were your class rankings, and it was just good at motivating boys. Boys really respond to competition. Now the schools have become so noncompetitive. They complain about boys playing video games, but with games, you have to compete, you have to achieve, and you get rewarded. In schools, it's no longer like that. Boys' schools are helpful, at least they were to me. I got along better with the teachers there because I was just bored a lot of the time. I was a high achiever. The woman teachers would all take me out in the hall and say, 'I'm so disappointed in you. How could you do this?' I was just making smart alecky comments and they would just take it so personally. It was much easier with male teachers. They didn't take it personally. There might be discipline but there wasn't the personal disappointment.

"The girls at Yale when I went there in 1971 were some of the first classes with women, and the ratio of girls to guys was lopsided with girls being hit on by guys constantly since there were so few of them. The guys finally just stopped trying and most of them never had girlfriends. The guys went on strike because most of the girls got such an attitude. Many were wall-flowers in high school but now they were being sought after. Before the coed days, it was easier to get dates because the guys would meet women at the girls' schools and vice versa." Jack's point is that if there are a lot of guys vying for the same women, like on the dating apps, it makes it harder to find someone who is relationship material. So what do you do?

Advice for Men

"My advice now to middle-aged guys would be to look for women over thirty. because in their twenties, everyone is after them. And also after my first marriage. when I was dating, one of my bachelor friends also told me to look for women in the South. New York women are too hard. You've really got to go elsewhere for a wife. I have always thought about that. You want someone smart, obviously, but you also need someone who hasn't bought into this feminist stuff too. So maybe go find someone from the South.

"As a writer, I had bought into all this feminist stuff when I was younger. When I was at Yale, all the women wanted to be doctors and professionals and I thought 'great, if they want to do that stuff, I'll be a writer and marry someone like that.' But in my twenties and thirties, I noticed my friends were marrying women who were very successful in their career and then once they got married, the women lost interest in their careers and the guys were going to be the breadwinner. You might have thought you weren't but you were. I bought into the whole thing. My mother was a PhD after having four kids and had a career teaching school and then became an administrator. I was used to women working but I started to see it doesn't always work out this way."

So perhaps Jack's point here is not to take the things women *say* they want as necessarily true, but rather look at what they do. Does your girlfriend help out after you have been dating a while or does she look to you to pay for and take care of everything, all the while talking about being a feminist? If she likes to work and helps out, you know you have a gem. But if her finances are hers and *your* finances are hers, perhaps it is time to move on. The problem here sometimes is that if you get a feminine woman who wants to stay home, and you are the primary breadwinner, you may be the primary loser in a divorce.

Jack told me about a story he wrote on a meeting of guys who had lost custody of their kids, and the stories were just awful. "I remember one guy said to me that his wife came back from seeing a lawyer because they were splitting up and she threw a plate at the ground. He thought 'fuck you' and threw a plate on the ground too. She called the police and he was out of the house. Another guy asked me 'do you have a kid?' And when I said 'yes,' he said 'if your wife wanted, you would never see that kid again or at least not for years.' It was really harrowing and it had a big impact on me. I think that's why your book is so important, because of stories like these. And also, this men on strike thing is real. When I see these big organizations where they aren't promoting men anymore, my reaction to that is just go off and do something on your own."

"I believe that," I said to Jack. "If things don't work for men, many will go out and find a way to make it on their own or take matters into their own hands." I thought about the fraternity guys in the earlier section of this book who are action-oriented and don't let the administrations or faculty get them down. Men are resilient. So are you if you are reading this book.

My next interviewee, Sergio, has more to say on this resilience and how important it is for men to persevere in love and work in today's anti-male climate in order to find a happy life. He is a tall, successful medical doctor who learned the hard way that women who say they want a tall, successful man with money often turn on you in the end. Yet, like some of the other men I interviewed, he stayed with his first wife, even though she betrayed him time and time again. He has advice for younger men on how to find the right woman before this happens to them. "I didn't know love until I finally found my third wife, Rebecca. There is nothing more important."

Sergio

"Find a woman you would take a bullet for."

The first thing Sergio told me is that he is Armenian and is very proud of his culture and his family. He is a tall, handsome seventy-three-year-old who started a large and successful medical practice years ago. He recently retired and graciously agreed to be interviewed. I asked him about his background, and he said his grandfathers grew up in Armenia.

"My dad was the first born in the United States. I grew up in Pittsburgh. Both of my grandfathers were in the Armenian genocide in 1915. The grandfather I am named for was active against the Turks in the genocide. He was told that the Turks were coming to kill him and he fled to America. The Turks would come into the villages and give the Christian Armenian men the chance to convert to Islam. The men who didn't were either killed on the spot or were put in the front lines against the British army to let their bullets kill them. My grandfather had been married to my grandmother, but she was captured. The women and children were left to starve in the Syrian desert, but my grandmother escaped and was pregnant at that time with my mother. My grandparents didn't see each other for six years and then found each other again.

"My grandfather went to Pittsburgh, Pennsylvania, where a number of Armenians lived. He found his wife again later through a personal ad put in a newspaper and she brought their daughter to the US. My father was an Army medic who survived numerous wars. We have a lot of family history.

"I have a younger brother and we always talk about how blessed we were to be raised by my parents. It was the 50s. We were never wealthy, we were middle-class. While I was growing up, dad worked as a businessman who put out fires in a drafting and engineering supply company. I went to four high schools in four states. That would be called child abuse today but it made me very adaptable. Dad was the breadwinner, mom was at home. Our house was filled with classical music. My mom signed us up for every lesson possible trying to make civilized men out of these two barbarians. Once when we broke a window with a baseball, mom made us clean all dad's shoes to keep him calm and said, 'just wait until your dad gets home.' He wasn't really all that mad, it was just the thought of what he might do.

"I was the first-born grandson and my grandfather was the one who determined my career. He was a big deal in the

Armenian community in Pittsburgh and everyone looked up to him. He looked at my mom and said, 'make this one a doctor.' It was very patriarchal at that time. I went to Notre Dame for college and then did a detour for medical school into the military. My dad's middle-class salary could pay for me and my brother to go to college, but he only had money for one of us to go to medical school. I said, 'you know Dad, I have always loved the military and I can go to med school that way. Give the money to my brother.' I went into the navy and was an ensign.

"I went to the University of Pittsburgh for medical school and was in an endocrinology rotation which was fascinating. But it took so long back then to get an answer from tests—like thirty days. So one day I was at Presbyterian Hospital and I walked by this dark room and this doctor said, 'hey kid, you want to see an ulcer?' He had a fiber optic endoscope and he showed me the ulcer. He could make a diagnosis that fast. I loved the field after that experience because it is both cognitive and procedural. You use your brain and your hands, like you would in cardiology."

Relationships and Marriages

Sergio met his first fiancée at Notre Dame while in college. "That place was in northern Indiana, all-male at that time, and not a damn thing to do. Once football season was over and the snow fell, it was miserable, one of God's hellholes. My senior year, the school went coed. I had gone sophomore year without a single date. I became obsessed with girls. You think 'they're like up here, unattainable.' I remember our freshman mixer was at this all-girls' school across the street, Saint Mary's College. I watched this one girl who was fat and unattractive with acne sitting in the middle of a group of guys at this thing, talking about her appendectomy and these guys were hanging on her every word. No one could get a date." (Does this sound familiar? Online dating sounds similar for men today; women in their twenties have tons of guys after them and the guys that age are pretty much left out in the cold.)

"I met this gorgeous girl at Notre Dame while she was taking classes there from Saint Mary's. Students could cross over and take classes at either place. Saint Mary's was much less rigorous than Notre Dame. She wrote her first essay in a Notre Dame course on how to put on makeup and the professor told her that if this was her real life, her grade was an F. But if it was satire, she got an A. She was my fiancée for a while but her dad had oil wells or something. Her parents were Catholic and wanted our kids to be raised Catholic, and wanted me to move to Kansas to go to medical school. My fiancée was just sitting there saying nothing. I should have said something but didn't. She went to Europe for the summer and I broke up with her after that. But then it was from the frying pan into the fire.

"My dad always had us working physical jobs during the summers, but this particular summer after I finished college, he told me that I could work a nonphysical job at a department store. That's where I met Sharon. She was in college and this was her summer job too."

"What did you like about her?" I asked.

"The sex. Remember, I was at Notre Dame for four years at an all-male school, and if you are, like me, a congenital skirt chaser, an all-male school is great because there is nothing else to do. So I got married. I should have paid attention to my dad though. A month before we got married, my dad told me it was a bad idea, that she was pretty much dirt poor which troubled him. He offered me $20,000 not to marry her. Remember this was in the 1970's and Dad was really just middle-class. My parents saw something. They said, 'she is not right for you, she's not good for you. It won't end well.' But I said, 'Oh, Dad, I love her.'

"I should have known from the get-go that she was trouble. My birthday was July 1, and I started an internship and she left me for my birthday to go off with friends. We had a lot of issues. It turned out she had been unfaithful during our engagement. But I married her anyway. It affected me for years and I really didn't trust her. We did have two wonderful children, a son and daughter I love so much. We were married twenty-six years."

At this point, I asked Sergio a question I had always been curious about, "Why do doctors often have bad wives?"

"I wouldn't generalize," he said. "I had a happy childhood and wanted a wonderful marriage like my parents had." But then he thought about it and said, "My sister-in-law came to me after my first wife and I divorced and said, 'I should have told you this but I asked Sharon on your wedding day why she wanted to marry you and she said 'I want to marry a doctor because they make a lot of money and are never around.'" I guess this answered my question as to why some women want doctors, kind of like why women marry prisoners—you know where they are and they don't get in the way. "We went through therapy but it didn't help," Sergio said.

"What was she like?" I asked.

"She was selfish and entitled. My God, it was impossible to make her happy. This is really embarrassing to talk about but I gave her the world. I would even take her parents to Hawaii, on cruises. On one birthday she wanted me to pay for her sister and her brother-in-law to go to Italy. I paid for everything. At one point on the trip, we went to a lovely restaurant where I paid cash for the bill. We left after a great meal and the owner ran after me and said, 'You didn't pay the bill!' 'I did pay the bill with a one hundred note and I left extra for a generous tip,' I said. The owner said there was no large bill in his till and I thought, 'maybe somebody grabbed the cash off the table.' And then my sister-in-law's husband said, 'Are you looking for this?' and pulls a one hundred euro note out of his pocket. 'I took it,' he said. 'I thought you left too much.' I grabbed it from him and gave it to the owner and said, 'I am so sorry.' Here I was paying for everyone in my wife's family and he took a one hundred euro note off the table? And hell, no, he wasn't going to give it back to me. These are the sorts of things they would do.

"I put up with this behavior for twenty-six years because in my family, we don't believe in divorce. We went to therapy when she wanted a divorce, and I told my wife, 'I don't want this, it will mess up our lives and our children's lives and our grandkids lives'. The kids were in college then. I was even willing to have a platonic relationship."

At this point, it was hard for me to fathom why *anyone* would stay in such a relationship and I asked Sergio why it was so important to stay married. "Shame," he said. Men are conditioned to believe that they're always the bad guy and some will do anything to keep face with their family and friends. We always hear that women are "people pleasers" who are victims, but Sergio's behavior is an extremely common example of how men allow themselves to be mistreated in relationships, and rather than move on, they use money and groveling as a way to hold onto a distant mate who doesn't want them. This never works. Sergio continued to hang onto the relationship but it finally ended when reality hit him in the face.

"My wife was kind of out there, into yoga and other stuff like Qigong. At one point she told me she was going to Australia with her Qigong instructor. She thought this guy was a guru and he told her she had special powers. 'He says I am very talented.' I was like, 'What are you talking about?' My wife told me that her instructor warned her about my reaction and said 'doctors don't believe this kind of stuff.' 'I said, are you out of your mind? You are married, you can't go off with this guy.' She said 'Yes, I can' and left. She filed divorce papers a month before she went.

"I called a lawyer and he told me to cut off her credit cards because 'her and her boyfriend will be using them to pay for their honeymoon at my expense.' I retorted back to him, 'That's not her boyfriend.' He said, 'wake up and smell the coffee, cut off the credit cards.' So I did and she called me and said 'You bastard, what is wrong with you, don't you care about your kids? How can I buy stuff for them?' Like an idiot, I said, 'You're right, I'm sorry.'" At this point, Sergio looked at me and said, "I know, it's my problem that I gave her back the cards. She used them to fund a trip for her and this guy. But the funny thing is as soon as they got back, he dumped her. Thank God, our divorce came final on April Fool's Day of 2004.

"My ex got 55 percent of everything. My attorney, Sally, said, 'Even though Tennessee is not a community property state, all the chancellors here behave as if it is, and it doesn't matter that she cheated on you or even if she had sex with the Sixth Fleet on a bridge, it still doesn't matter.' My choices were to give her 50/50 and pay alimony until she is sixty-five or pay her 55 percent without alimony, so I took the latter.

"Even after my divorce, I wanted to be married again." "Why?" I asked. "Because I loved being married, I loved having kids. I only went on two dates after that. One was with a Jewish woman and I thought we really hit it off. But I mentioned to her that I liked *Seinfeld* and she got upset and said, 'he is anti-Semitic.' I said, 'but he's Jewish.' She held to her position and I was like, 'that was the end of that evening.' I wasn't upset, I just figured our sense of humor was just different. The next date I went on was with a very sexy woman that someone fixed me up with. She came dressed like she was going to a strip club. I'm not a prude but she just wanted to have sex and get married right off the bat. So that was that.

"This gets more embarrassing. There was a lovely nurse at my office, Angie, and she was very sweet. I asked her out—this was before there was a policy in the office against such things. She was very attractive and had a great sense of humor. We dated for eighteen months before we got married. She had two girls, nine and thirteen. The marriage was ok but it became obvious in the marriage that I was third fiddle. The girls hated their own father and as the teen got older, she had issues; she was promiscuous. This caused issues between us but nothing major.

"As for my second marriage ending, I blame entirely myself because a woman I had always been interested in became available. She was the most wonderful person I had ever met. Grace was my dermatologist and when she got divorced, I asked her ex-husband if he would mind if I asked her out. This was the first time in my life that I understood what love means. There is a saying I heard—love is if you would take a bullet for someone. Up until that point, I would only have taken a bullet for my children and my parents. But now I understand. How I wish I had met Grace first. We have so much in common, we both had moms who were artists, similar backgrounds. We would have had our own kids but we are thankful that we met when we did. I would have hated to have a woman like my first wife now and be heading into the grave with Satan.

"If I have one thing I feel guilty about is that I divorced my second wife who did nothing wrong. But for the first time in my life, when I married Grace, I did something for myself. I divide the world into givers and takers and I had been a giver all my life, and it is the first time I took something. We have been married thirteen wonderful years."

Thoughts on Feminism

I asked Sergio about how the feminist movement has changed since he was young. He said, "When I grew up, the feminist movement was coming along and I loved it, especially women's independence. That became the ideal, to be independent. But now the young women I see as patients—it's different. They are taking everything you all have earned and worked for—like you, you are independent, intelligent and hardworking. Now these young ones just want to be taken care of. Honestly, they dress like skanks and all they care about is finding a rich guy."

"Why do you think that is?" I asked.

"I guess TV and social media.

"I even know a few female professors who have teenage boys who have told me independently that they are going to have their sons spend the summers in France or Italy to find a French or Italian girl. They tell me they don't want the women in their classrooms as daughters-in-law. They say these girls are horrible people. They are drunks, promiscuous, they don't want to work hard, they just want a rich guy to take care of them. I find this interesting coming from women professors. I have seen what this entitled behavior does to men firsthand.

"At my work, people seem to love to open up to me—I guess my face looks friendly and kind. Let me tell you about one guy who was a patient who recently came to see me. He walked in and burst into tears. He is a big burly guy and said, 'My wife just left me and asked for a divorce.' I asked him what happened and he said, 'Doc, you're not going to believe this. My wife was married before and her ex recently got killed in a skiing accident, and he never took her off his life insurance. She got one million in life insurance from her ex-husband and she came to me and said, 'I never loved you, I just needed some place to stay and someone to pay my bills.' They were married for eighteen years and had a daughter and this is what she tells him. She could have said something less mean. My patient was devastated. It was like this hatred on her part." (This anecdote sounds very similar to what Myron Gaines said in his book, *Why Women Deserve Less*, where he talks about women just not liking men very much.)

"Do you think some women hate men?" I asked him. "Yes," he said with no hesitation. "I think the way things have progressed and changed in our society, there is this entitlement, in both sexes. But for women, I think they feel entitled that they will find someone rich—even my first ex was off at Martha's Vineyard and other places trying to find a rich guy, but she has never remarried in the past twenty years."

Women in Medicine

At the end of our interview, I asked Sergio to give me his insights into the growing entry of women in medicine. "What do you think about the fact that 38 percent of active physicians are now women?[106] How do you think this has changed the field—for better or worse?"

"I'm sorry to say this to you, but I think it has changed for the worse. The women don't work as much. Part of this is that they have children and they still have to do the majority of the childrearing responsibilities. Yes, they have children but they do not want to take calls, they choose other specialties like dermatology or radiology, they don't go into gastroenterology as often. [Around 19 percent of gastroenterologists are women currently and 30 percent of new trainees in the field are women.][107] Most of the women who are gastroenterologists want the clinic work, not the hospital work which is harder. When they graduate, they go right into a clinic so they can control their schedule with fewer hours. That's fine, I get it. It's not right or wrong. But I was on call every other night. Maybe I'm just a dinosaur but I worked 100 to 110 hours a week. That was insanity maybe." I mentioned to Sergio the studies that said patients had better outcomes with female doctors.[108] "Do you believe this?" I asked.

"No, I don't. Let me tell you give you an example. One of my former partners called me up to tell me that he was at a local hospital with two endoscopy rooms and one of the other doctors, a woman, was next door in the other room. My former partner said he had done three procedures while the woman

---

[106] Patrick Boyle, et al, "Women are changing the face of medicine in America," *AAMCNews*, May 28, 2024. https://www.aamc.org/news/women-are-changing-face-medicine-america

[107] "Supporting and Empowering Women Physicians," *GastroHealth Press Release*, September 6, 2022. https://gastrohealth.com/news/press-release/supporting-and-empowering-women-physicians

[108] Robert Hart, "Patients Fare Better With Women Doctors, Study Finds," *Forbes*, April 22, 2024. https://www.forbes.com/sites/roberthart/2024/04/22/patients-fare-better-with-women-doctors-study-finds/

had done one. He wondered what the issue was and sent a nurse over to find out if anything was wrong and the nurse came back saying there was a lesion that has been obstructed. The female doctor had called a surgeon down to help get through the lesion with emergency surgery because she could not get through this 'tumor.' Some of the staff came in the partner's room to get a smaller scope which was in his room. The staff asked him if he could give Dr. Cindy some help, so he said 'sure' and went to look at the screen to see what was going on. Dr. Cindy thought there was a tumor near the rectum, but it turned out, she was in the vagina, the cervix, not the rectum and didn't know the difference. There was no tumor. This is a true story.

"I think many doctors just don't get the training they need with patients these days—they use AI classes or other means and really need more training with actual people because it is different. But this is a conversation for a whole other book."

Advice for Young Men

"Don't Settle."

"Before we end, do you have any advice for younger men?" I asked "I think this young generation of men has wised up about what is happening in marriage. They have seen their dad, uncle, or brother go through a lot. My advice is 'don't settle, take your time to find the right person.'" "How do you know the right person?" I asked. "Do they give as much as they take?" he said. "This sounds so simple," I thought, "but it isn't." In our society, men are expected give protection, affection, financial support, and a host of other things in a relationship, and women are told that they are enough as they are—they give too much already.

This is a myth for the most part but one that many men have swallowed.

If you want happiness in a relationship, ask yourself if she gives as much as she takes. If the answer is "yes," you are a lucky guy. If the answer is "no," think long and hard about whether this should be a permanent relationship. Sergio's experience with his first marriage (and Charlie's in the chapter before) should be a lesson that it is better to end up later in life with the right woman than earlier in life with the wrong one.

CHAPTER SEVEN

Themes and Takeaways

A t this point, after reading over the men's accounts of their lives, you may be thinking, what do we do now? What have we learned from all this, and how can individuals make things better for themselves, and how can society at large make things better for men and boys? While there is no clear cut answer for everybody, there are some themes and takeaways that I will explore to gain more understanding of how to help.

Here are the consistent themes I found when I analyzed these men's lives stories:

1. **Men Love Women.** First and foremost, the majority of the men I interviewed loved women and were hesitant to say anything negative about them. Even the college men described women in loving terms, like "How could you not love them? Men were made to love women," and so forth. However, the college men did have concerns about their relationships and questioned

whether their liberal girlfriends would ever have the same values as themselves.

2. **Fatherless men lack confidence.** The men who were fatherless or had a poor relationship with their dad were missing something and had more trouble with relationships and dating. Those with positive male father figures did better in life and were more successful, with women, at work, and even on the dating apps. These positive role models were often a stepfather who took an interest in them when young and showed them what it was to be a man who loved his family.

3. **Men lack male role models.** Whether it is at school, work, or society at large, many of the men who were least successful had few male role models to help them navigate the world. Men who went to all male schools seemed to fare the best and mentioned how much they learned from being around boys and men. The men I interviewed contradicted the studies researchers like Reeves say show that male-sex schools are not helpful.

4. **Men who moved often as kids had more anxiety and stress as a result.** This was an important theme throughout the book for some of the men, that moving to a new school environment and neighborhood was harder on them than for their sisters. Having to prove yourself to a new group of friends and being the new kid was very difficult for some of the men. This was especially true for those men who had grown up without a father figure in their lives.

5. **Men feel that they do not live up to women's standards and expectations.** In today's world, boys and men are surrounded by women from nursery school to

healthcare to marriage where they are told they do not measure up. Colleges are almost 60 percent women[109] and the men's needs are not seen as a priority. Dating apps give the edge to young women who often have more men to choose from and are much pickier than the men. The standards for dating become impossible to meet (six feet tall, six figure income, a six-pack, and the like.) and many men do not make the cut.

6. **Men feel that they are left to fend for themselves by family and the culture.** They have no safety net. Women have more support or are encouraged to be the best they can be. The men felt that women often vote for the government to benefit themselves which men find troubling, as they believe too much government intervention makes things worse. The men agreed that this lack of support meant that they had to take more risks to make it, though they were afraid of failure because no one would come to their aid. This fear of failure caused some men they knew to live at home, abuse substances or have trouble in their careers. Some of the men mentioned that their own fathers had experienced trouble with fear of failure and turned to self-destructive behavior as a result. Men mentioned fear of risk as a problem for many men.

7. **All the men mentioned having trouble finding a woman who was politically similar or who had similar values.** This is particularly true for the youngest

---

[109] "A Generation of Men Give Up on College: 'I just feel lost,'" Wall Street Journal, September 6, 2021. https://www.wsj.com/us-news/education/college-university-fall-higher-education-men-women-enrollment-admissions-back-to-school-11630948233

men. The fraternity men I talked with (ages twenty-one to twenty-two) all had liberal girlfriends and this was a concern for them in a future relationship. Women tended to be liberal and to feel that their views were most important. There were exceptions, but the men who were happiest were with women who shared similar values, even if they were politically different.

8. **Men are afraid of conflict with women and will do anything to avoid it.** Men of all ages were afraid to rock the boat in their relationships and speak their mind. This led to men withdrawing or becoming depressed—or worse, trying to placate a woman with gifts or money to keep her interested. The men who did best with women were the ones who set boundaries. This boundary-setting sometimes led to breakups or divorce, but the men's lives after divorce were often better due to peace while living on one's own terms or from finding a more suitable partner.

9. **Older men who were happy in later life had divorced a wife who was unsuitable.** They found a partner who was similar to themselves and shared their values. Happier older men also continued working, often in freelance work or at a job that they had held for years. Older men not in a relationship valued their job even more, as they felt they were providing a useful service for others. One man mentioned his job was like a family even though he was not paid particularly well. Another man found peace doing personal training on his own schedule and living by his own rules without a wife.

Finally, the most important point I found from my interviews was that:

10. **Men are opting out of the system rather than fighting back or standing up for themselves.** They are not trying to change the system. If a man is told at work that white middle-aged men will not be promoted, they simply kept their job without rocking the boat—usually because they liked the job. One interviewee mentioned that some men moved on to work on their own if they could. None mentioned a lawsuit or filing a discrimination suit. Another interviewee mentioned that the state came after him even though he paid child support; another was charged with false abuse allegations. There is a sense of helplessness about their situation—that nothing can be done.

But something can be done. When men stand for their rights, they can succeed but they need others to join them. We witnessed this first-hand at Madison Square Garden when Megyn Kelly decried a Trump rally was "too brotastic" because a lot of guys dared to come out to see Trump and Elon Musk[110]—many of the guys were young and had never been interested in politics or voting. Usually, the media vilifies young men as lazy and sitting in their basement playing video games, but when they do come out of the basement and get together, it's suddenly a negative "bro-fest." The real truth is that men banding together is threatening to those with a women-first agenda, and this is the case on both political sides of the aisle. It is no wonder men are discouraged from getting together. They might actually stand up for themselves or their communities

---

[110] Dominick Mastrangelo, "Megyn Kelly: Trump rally was 'too brotastic'," *The Hill*, October 29, 2024. https://thehill.com/homenews/media/4958952-megyn-kelly-trump-rally/

and demand a bigger megaphone. It will be interesting to see if the current presidential administration will provide better policies to help men succeed. I will discuss such policies in a later section, but first, here are some takeaways from the book that can help men to lead happier, more successful lives.

Takeaways

So, what have we learned so far about men's feelings and the themes that run through their lives in twenty-first century America? One thing I learned as I wrote this book is that men will easily speak about their lives if we are open to hearing them. And the themes these men shared with me were easily translated to steps the reader (and anyone concerned with men's health) can take if they want to see men flourish instead of flounder. Here are the highlights in no particular order of importance. (Hint—they are all important):

> *Step 1) If you learn nothing else from this book then at least learn this: "Don't listen when people discourage men from getting together." Meet with other men and talk about the issues that are of importance to you or just talk about guy stuff. We no longer have dedicated male spaces where men can go and talk freely to each other so you will need to make your own—it could be the gym, a political bro-fest, or pickup basketball or any other activity that is of interest to you. I see men at the gym having deep discussions, almost like peer-to-peer counseling. The men I interviewed who were the happiest had male friends they could turn to for help. Being that men are not*

as comfortable with therapy—and there are few therapists trained in men's issues, it is not a bad idea to talk with a guy (or guys) that you trust.

There are still good counselors out there—check out the Appendix to see what to look for if you decide you want professional treatment. I have a list of therapist qualities and suggestions to help you find a good professional if you decide you need one.

Step 2) If you want to make the world to a better place for men, for God's sakes, quit insulting men. And quit referring to men without women as "incels" or other derogatory terms. I shouldn't have to state the obvious but this step alone would probably fix 50 percent of today's relationships and depression in men, especially for those who are young and impressionable. And cut out adding "toxic" when addressing masculinity. Or if accused of toxic masculinity, at least don't try to placate the person saying it. One of my interviewees said that women he meets often tell him he has "toxic masculinity" to which he replies, "What did you expect? I'm a man who owns a concrete business and works with my hands." Best to own it.

Step 3) If you have a young son, don't move him around too much and have him change schools and think he will be okay without any assistance. Boys have a harder time moving and adjusting to new people than girls do. Warren Farrell discussed a study of 4500 families chosen randomly by the Department of Housing and Urban Development who moved to "better" neighborhoods. When the kids were studied fifteen years later, the rate of PTSD among boys who moved to better neighborhoods was like the rate found among soldiers returning from combat.[111] While this seems extreme, it turns out that when a boy moves, it is harder for him to feel comfortable with new male peers who often vet friends by testing them with teasing. This can lead to depression or acting out behavior for a new kid.[112] If you must move, keep a close eye on your son and have discussions with him at dinner or during activities to get a feel for how he is doing.

Step 4) Examine your emotions. Boys today are taught to come at problems ways similar to those that girls use to handle their issues. They are internalizing their problems more, and this has led to more men reacting with depression and anxiety. One of the interviewees mentioned that even the men he sees act overly emotional and scream and rant when upset. He attributed this behavior to boys seeing how single moms react and then copying similar behavior later in life. If you are reacting to situations by getting depressed

---

[111] Andrew M. Seaman, "Moving out of poverty linked to kids' mental health," *Reuters*, March 4, 2014. https://www.reuters.com/article/business/healthcare-pharmaceuticals/moving-out-of-poverty-linked-to-kids-mental-health-idUSBREA2324K/

[112] Farrell and Gray, *The Boy Crisis*, 265.

or anxious or with emotional lability, either get treatment or write down what situations get you upset or angry and work on coping by being more direct and calm in making your needs known.

Step 5) Learn to take some risks in your life but not in destructive ways. Drinking too much and engaging in fights is not typically constructive. The men I interviewed who were successful went out on a limb, reached out to find something that made them feel worthwhile and gave them a sense of purpose. One started his own health business even while admitting to feeling afraid, another finally went after a woman he desired rather than ones that desired him, some left marriages that were toxic, and yet others fought hard for their kids and won custody even with the odds against them.

I spoke to one thirty-seven-year-old man who said he "hired an aggressive female lawyer and got 50/50 custody of his son." He did not back down and miraculously was not ordered to pay additional child support. Research shows that men will often back down when it comes to fighting for custody and this is why they lose their kids. Don't be one of them. Men are getting custody more now than in the past due to a number of factors.[113] Other men in the interviews took risks by asking for what they wanted in a relationship or by not avoiding conflict with a woman which leads to the next step.

---

[113] "More Men are Winning Custody Disputes: Here's Why," Dwire Law Offices, P.A., January 20, 2017. https://www.divorceminnesota.com/blog/2017/01/more-men-are-wining-custody-disputes-heres-why/

Step 6) Learn to tolerate conflict in a relationship and try not to withdraw as a first response. You may have to ask your wife or girlfriend to give you time to process information, let them know how you feel directly or tell her if she is overly critical or not giving you the respect you would like. It is hard to do this and takes practice. Men are often afraid that if they speak up, they will make things worse or be abandoned. However, if you never speak up about what is bothering you and accept everything in silence, the relationship is not healthy anyway. And if telling your partner what you need is met with hostility, insults or criticism, it is time to rethink why you are still with her. At the same time, you must give a person time to understand how you feel.

For example, your wife tells you that you don't help out enough. You get annoyed and don't talk much or worse, you acquiesce and try to placate her by going overboard. Neither of these approaches is helpful. The later will make you angry and resentful and the former will not resolve anything if silence is your answer. Try to meet in the middle and ask her for specifics and work on those. If she doesn't acknowledge this or just asks for more, let her know how you feel. "I did the dishes but you said that I am still not helping enough. What is a good way to resolve this?" If your partner insults or denigrates you, that is a different story and you should not tolerate such disrespect. This is one case where it best to speak up directly and tell her that you will not tolerate insults or disrespect.

Step 7) Finally—and of great importance—own your masculinity. Do not let women or society tell you that somehow you are bad, toxic, or entitled for being male. This is a destructive cognitive belief meant to spread like a virus to rob men of their confidence, sense of purpose, and even a desire to live. Men who commit suicide have feelings of despair that come from feeling worthless. Depression will not improve if men are told they are worthless. Negative feelings towards men is toxic, not being male. Stand your ground and believe that men are free agents who can choose their own path—particularly one that focuses on masculine pursuits. Engage in daily activities that you find rewarding such as target practice, sports, games that demand competition or something similar, and merit-based work—and don't apologize to anyone for it.

Guiding Principles for Government and Society

There are a number of ways that government and society can improve the lives of men and boys. I will point out the top contenders using the interviews and suggestions from the men themselves in the previous chapters.

1. *We need more male teachers and male role models in schools and in society at large.* Some researchers, such as Reeves, are not fans of single-sex schools. He says it is better to have coed schools where teachers and staff

are taught how to improve the learning and health of boys by revising teacher education courses to include some of the scientific evidence on sex differences.[114] He mentions the work of Michael Gurian, who believes that boys and girls learn differently.[115] My husband and I did a podcast with Gurian in 2006 on how boys learn, and he is an amazing advocate for boys.[116] He mentions that single sex schools help both aggressive boys and sensitive boys in an all-male environment do better.[117] I believe this is the case from the men I spoke with who felt good about their all-male schools and definitely recommended them to others. That said, all-male schools are not right for every boy, of course, so coed schools should be trained in specific techniques that help all boys learn. Public schools should have this training and female teachers in particular should learn how to interact with boys to help them succeed in a less biased environment.

2. *Stop the public denigration of men and boys.* This is a cultural change that should be encouraged in school systems through teacher and college administrators' training in the schools. Or better yet, get rid of administrators or departments whose main function is to discriminate against men. The verbal abuse of men and

---

[114] Reeves, *Of Boys and Men,* 148–149.

[115] Michael Gurian and Patricia Henley with Terry Trueman, *Boys and Girls Learn Differently! A Guide for Teachers and Parents* (Jossey-Bass, San Francisco, 2001).

[116] You can hear the podcast at https://instapundit.com/wp-content/uploads/podcasts/GlennHelenPodcast--GurianandMeigs.mp3

[117] Michael Gurian, "Benefits of a Single-Gender Education," YouTube, November 3, 2016. https://www.youtube.com/watch?v=9irG52saVYI

boys in schools and in the media has set up a toxic environment where men are portrayed as ADHD-riddled potential rapists who need constant supervision. The commercials where men are viewed as a bumbling bunch of idiots seem to be receding somewhat since I wrote *Men on Strike* over ten years ago. However, these types of commercials should be discouraged, and complaints levied if they contain damaging portrayals of men and boys.

3. *Due process and the right to a hearing should be permanently restored to colleges* for those (mostly men) who are accused of sexual harassment. Under the Biden-era Title IX rules, accused students lost "their right to a guaranteed live hearing with the opportunity to have a representative cross-examine their accuser. This is accompanied by a return to the 'single-investigator model,' which allows a single administrator to investigate and decide the outcome of a case."[118] No one should have that much power. As of January, 2025, the Trump administration restored laws to make them more equitable for those accused. "That includes the right of both parties to have lawyers present during hearings, the right for both attorneys to cross-examine the other party and witnesses, and the right to receive all of the evidence in the institution's possession."[119]

---

[118] Emma Camp, "New Title IX Rules Erase Campus Due Process Protections," *Reason*, April 19, 2024. https://reason.com/2024/04/19/new-title-ix-rules-erase-campus-due-process-protections/

[119] "Crucial due process rights for America's college students," *FIRE*, January 31, 2025. https://www.thefire.org/news/statement-trump-restores-crucial-due-process-rights-americas-college-students

4. *Older teens and men need more resources for higher learning*, both at the college level and for technical and vocational training. Technical training should start in high school and should be emphasized more for those boys who want to work in the trades. In higher education, there could be a two-tiered system at freestanding technical schools, and at universities for those interested in a higher four-year degree. Even the college men I interviewed thought that universities should incorporate programs in-house so that men who are interested in the trades could get a college degree with a focus on their trade, along with business and marketing. There is not enough funding for technical schools or scholarships in general for men. That needs to change.

5. *Get rid of DEI.* It is no friend to men and creates a hostile environment, particularly for those who don't fit the appropriate ethnic group. This is already happening with the new Trump administration which is working to put an end to these programs that discriminate unfairly due to sex and ethnicity. Bring back merit-based hiring.

6. *Bring back more jobs in manufacturing and areas that have been lost to globalization.* Men's wages and psyches have suffered from a lack of higher paying jobs and been replaced with a credentialed class that tells men that they can't get ahead without a college degree, even in fields where degrees aren't necessary. Some states are already getting rid of some of the requirements for a college degree.[120] Other states should follow suit.

---

[120] Ungar-Sargon, *Second Class*, 138.

7. *Provide more single-sex schools, particularly for boys.*
School choice for parents should be on the agenda so
that parents can find schools that are right for their
kids. Large public schools can be hard for boys to
maneuver in, and boys are more likely to get depressed
or have issues in large anonymous settings.

For the Women

I started this book thinking it would be of interest mostly to
men but as I talked to more and more women, I realized that
many are at a loss when it comes to helping (or even understanding) boyfriends, husbands and sons. In general, our society and other women will not tell you the truth about how
to get along with the men in your life. If you want to have a
better relationship with men, try the following tips and see if
you don't get a better response, and learn more about the men
in your life at the same time.

1. First, *listen and realize that men have feelings*. If this
book teaches you nothing else, just remember that men
will talk if you are willing to listen and understand
without making the conversation about you. They
may say things you don't like to hear. Try to be open to
hearing them. I have even witnessed women slapping
men because "they are bigger than me and it doesn't
hurt." It does, and so do emotional slings and arrows
that women believe don't wound men. They often do.
Remember Joey in the episode of *Friends* where his
girlfriend hit him constantly and insisted it didn't hurt?

He was reluctant to tell her and it caused problems in the relationship.[121]

2. *Stay positive if you ask a man to help around the house and he tries.* It may not be up to your standards but give praise for trying. Remember that just because he isn't great at the dishes, he often picks up medicine for the kids or helps you with your car (or whatever else that he does for you).

3. *Do not use your girlfriends for advice about your husband's feelings or denigrate him and men to them.* Ask him in a caring way when he is not under stress how he feels or how you can resolve an issue.

4. *Pay as much attention to your sons' feelings and mental health as that of your daughters.* I often talk to moms who tell me all about their daughters, what they are doing, how successful they are, and so forth. Occasionally, they will bring up the son (that I never even knew about) as an afterthought. I even had one mom who referred to her son as an "asshole." Maybe he was, but this view is not going to encourage better behavior. Women, in particular, feel very free to say what is on their minds to their son, thinking he is not listening. He is. Do not denigrate boys and men in front of him—and behind his back isn't great either.

5. *If you have a son, be very aware of his feelings if you have to move neighborhoods.* He may not say anything, but talk to him prior to the move and keep in touch with him at dinner or during activities to get his view on how things are going at school, and with making new

---

[121] "The One with the Girl Who Hits Joey," Wikipedia. https://en.wikipedia.org/wiki/The_One_with_the_Girl_Who_Hits_Joey

friends after the move. If you have to change schools for your son's sake, do it if at all possible. I talked with a grandfather who said his sensitive ten-year-old grandson attended a middle school where there was fighting (mainly between girls) and there were no doors on the bathroom for privacy. He was miserable until the parents sent him to a private school where such behavior was not tolerated. This boy is now happy and doing well. It may take sacrifice, but helping your son to learn in a better environment is worth the effort.

6. *Don't say bad things about his father or men in general in front of your son.* Of course this is not possible 100 percent of the time, but make a conscious effort not to do this, especially if you are divorced.

7. *Make sure if you are divorced to have positive male role models for your son.* This could be a step-father, teacher or uncle, but it is imperative for most boys. Try to keep his own dad involved in his life as much as possible unless it is harming your son's mental or physical health to be with him.

8. *Finally, if you make more money than your partner, don't use that as leverage against him.* Try to be open to the idea that spouses/partners help each other and money is but a tool to do that. This is not to say that he shouldn't pay his fair share or take on responsibilities at home if you are the major breadwinner but it does mean that respect is still key. If there is a single thing that men are most short of in relationships, it is that—respect.

Conclusion

"Men want to be accepted, not fixed."

"He has mommy issues," she said, as her nails were being painted and tended to by the technician at my local nail salon. As I noted earlier in the book, the topic of men and dating had started a conversation in the salon I go to once the women heard me tell my nail tech what I was writing about. The women all felt very free to speak up on their views of men. Any men in the area kept quiet—though to be fair, there weren't many there. Several women joined in to give me their opinions, and the woman next to me, a late thirties social worker described her current dating situation. Figuring a psychologist writing a book on men would be empathetic to her plight, she asked "Why do men only give 25 percent in a relationship?" My response, "maybe because women only give 10 percent" was met with a mixture of surprise and uncertainty about how to proceed. I reminded myself not to be a smart ass and learn something, and asked her about her current boyfriend. "He hasn't called me for three weeks," she said. "We were getting along and I thought it was serious."

"Did something happen?" I asked.

"Yes, I introduced him to my four kids and I haven't heard much from him since," she said, and proceeded to show me pictures of four adorable children. "I don't know why he can't commit to anything. Although his mother did abandon him and his fiancée left him at the altar. I think he has mommy issues."

Let's dissect this conversation. The first thing this woman does is make an insult about men in general—they only give 25 percent. Then she proceeds to say that the man she is seeing for not that long is not talking to her as much since meeting her four kids. Four kids is a *lot* to spring on someone. But rather than understand the ramifications of a man being involved with a woman with numerous children, she insults him further. "He must have mommy issues." When it comes to men having feelings and their own thoughts and lives, women just don't get it. Women often view men as utilitarian objects rather than human beings. What women don't understand and don't care to understand is that most men want to be accepted, not fixed or insulted.

Case in point: I was talking to a twenty-seven-year-old woman recently who asked me for relationship advice when she found out I had been married for thirty years. I told her to be positive and try not to make negative comments when it came to her boyfriend. She said, "Oh yeah, men are like children, aren't they?" "No," I told her. "They are human beings. Imagine your boyfriend said, 'oh, yeah, women just aren't that smart.' How would you feel?" "Not good at all, bad actually." "Yes, remember that when you think of saying something negative to your boyfriend." To her credit, she nodded and seemed to understand. Will she carry it out? I don't know but at least if she understands her part in making a relationship work, she might try. In our current "you go girl" society, women are given no direction in how to talk to men other than to belittle or blame them for their failings or even for their politics. If no one calls these women out and they get no input from others, nothing will change. And it may not even be their fault; they have no role models that have shown them anything better. The media and social media confirm their worst feelings about men and do nothing but exacerbate the problem.

I challenge any reader of this book to speak up next time a woman (or man, for that matter) denigrates men. In his latest book, Jonathan Haidt mentioned a 1968 psychology study showing that most people will *not* speak up even when smoke is filling a room if other people don't speak up first because they figure everything must be fine even if it is not.[122] Don't look around for confirmation that it is okay to say something, do it because it is the right thing to do. In our small way, maybe we can reach one person at a time or at least let them know that they cannot freely go after men without pushback or transparency about what they are doing. So speak up and don't just sit back and let the misandry fill the room.

Our society needs men who are strong and happy with life, not weak men who are treated as second-class citizens. Our society is becoming less productive as a result, but the worst part is that people's relationships have truly suffered. Men cannot find women who love them as human beings and women cannot find men they value. Ironically, dating, relationships, and life should lie beyond politics, but we cannot make them work without addressing the political and societal problems that are keeping men and women apart. We must all strive to give *both* men and women a voice at the table, for without both sexes having a say, neither sex will win.

---

[122] Haidt, *The Anxious Generation*, 291.

RESOURCES

Men's Retreat: Casas Kismet, Nosara, Guanacaste, Costa Rica. The Balanced Man Retreat is an exclusive opportunity uniquely designed for men seeking an unparalleled journey to rediscover themselves and reconnect with the inherent strength of masculinity in balance with empathy, compassion, and holistic well-being.

https://www.casaskismet.com/

Websites:

The Art of Manliness—https://www.artofmanliness.com/. This is a website run by Brett and Kate McKay that has some good podcasts and advice for men who want to hone their skills and learn how to manage life as a man in twenty-first century America.

Dr. Warren Farrell—https://warrenfarrell.com/. This website contains all of Dr. Farrell's books and appearances on men and boys in one place.

Captain Capitalism—http://captaincapitalism.blogspot.com/. This is a website run by Aaron Clarey who writes about men, economics, and how to become a Renaissance man.

Stephen Baskerville—https://www.stephenbaskerville.com/. This website contains the books and articles of Professor Baskerville.

Starting Strength—https://startingstrength.com/. This site showcases the work of Mark Rippetoe and teaches men (and women) how to lift weights and build their body with good form. There is an excellent podcast show on the site hosted by Rippetoe to teach both weightlifting basics and more complex moves.

The College Fix—https://www.thecollegefix.com/. This site works with college-age writers with the purpose of identifying and supporting young people who seek to improve campus journalism. They often point out discrimination against men in their articles.

The Gurian Institute—https://gurianinstitute.com/. This site focuses on the work of Michael Gurian, the author of *The Wonder of Boys*, who researches how boys and girls learn differently.

Books:

The Boy Crisis: Why Our Boys Are Struggling and What We Can Do About It by Warren Farrell and John Gray. This book explains why fathers and male role models are so important for boys.

Of Boys and Men: Why the Modern Male is Struggling, Why it Matters, and What to Do About It by Richard V. Reeves. This book excels at explaining some of the structural problems that face men in our society.

Manhood: The Masculine Virtues America Needs by Josh Hawley. While this book is positive about men's attributes and need for a sense of purpose, it does have a "white knight flavor," but it is still recommended if you are looking for a positive read about men.

Why Women Deserve Less by Myron Gaines and edited by Aaron Clarey. This book is the best eighty-six pages of material about the current online dating scene for men in America. The first page states, "It [the book] is to prevent you from wasting your resources on the unreciprocated romantic pursuit of women to the point it ruins your life." There are some men who need to hear this information in a straight, no-nonsense manner.

The Anxious Generation: How the Great Rewiring of Childhood is Causing an Epidemic of Mental Illness by Jonathan Haidt. This book examines rates of depression and anxiety in kids and has a chapter specifically on boys called "What is Happening to Boys?" He laments that boys are withdrawing from the real world and discusses why. Though I don't agree with some of his analysis, it is interesting and a good starting point to understand some of the dynamic that boys are dealing with in today's female-centered world. His chart on the declining of risk-taking for boys on page 182 is definitely worth a look.

Atomic Habits: An Easy & Proven Way to Build Good Habits & Break Bad Ones by James Clear. This book gives a clear and concise program to transform the habits that are holding you back and gives you the tools and techniques to achieve your own idea of success in small incremental steps. I think men will appreciate the straight-forward nature of the book and the writing, and use it to cope with procrastination or fear of failure.

Starting Strength: Basic Barbell Training by Mark Rippetoe. If you want to learn more about lifting and growing strong and want a great training guide, this book fits the bill. "Unlike other popular exercise protocols, *Starting Strength* is a training system—a long-term process designed for getting stronger over time."[123] My husband has followed this method and it has helped him gain strength and muscle over the years.

---

[123] Rippetoe, Mark Starting Strength Basic Barbell Training, third edition, The Aasgaard Company, 2011.

APPENDIX

How does a man find a good therapist?

B elow are some of my suggestions on what to look for if you decide you want professional treatment:

1. The best way to find a good therapist is word of mouth. You might ask other men or a woman you trust for recommendations, or ask your insurance company to match you with someone who specializes in your specific problem. If possible, see a male therapist who works well with men; but rather than gender, it is more important to find a therapist who respects men and understands their issues.

2. Once you call for an appointment, pay attention to how you are treated on the phone. Does the therapist call you back promptly if you leave a voicemail? Or does his/her staff act courteous over the phone? Arrange a first meeting to see how you get along with the therapist. You are after all, trying to interview and find out

if this professional is right for you. If the therapist is good, they will feel the same way. I let clients know that the first few sessions are a trial period to see if we can work together. If not, I give them three names of other psychologists who might be better for them.

3. Remember that the most important ingredient in patient change is a feeling that the therapist likes you. If you sense that there is no real connection with the therapist or the therapist seems to deal in generalities such as "men are this way, women that way," you should bring your concerns up in the first few sessions and discuss them to determine whether or not you should continue—which brings me to our fourth point.

4. Do not be intimidated by the therapist's PhD or MD. It does not give them license to hold their degree out as a reason you should listen to them. Listen to the words of your therapist and see if they are beneficial to you, or just downright silly or ineffective. Once a therapist says something like, "Listen to me because I have such and such degree," you might want to be heading for the door. This is not to say that degrees and training aren't helpful—they are, as hopefully your doctor has a good range of experience with those who have similar problems. But it is the knowledge they have to deal with your problem that is important, of course, not just the fact that they made it through school. Sharing with you their degrees and experience in a form or verbally at the beginning of therapy is normal.

5. Finally, if you are in therapy and you feel that no progress is being made, address it with the therapist and listen to the feedback. None of us is past interpreting our

problems incorrectly, and it may just be a misunder-
standing or miscommunication between you and the
therapist. Give him or her a chance to help you change
these misperceptions. But if that nagging feeling con-
tinues that you are not getting the help you need or the
therapist does not like you/respect you, it may be time
to consider a change.

6. More specifically, if you feel the therapist is biased
against men, bring it up directly and give him/her a
chance to change their approach. If they do not, it
is best to move on. But sometimes a therapist needs
feedback from you. One of my interviewees said that
the therapist sided with the wife. Rather than let the
therapist know how he felt, he "sat back and never
said another word." Speak up and see if the therapist
changes his or her behavior—but if not, at least it gives
you practice in being direct about your feelings and
need for respect and for your voice to be heard.

If you want to find a qualified professional in your area, the
National Register of Health Service Providers might be a good
place to start. Here's their website: https://www.findapsycholo-
gist.org/.

ACKNOWLEDGMENTS

Thanks to Glenn, Julia and James for all the deep discussions on men over the years and for the encouragement, nonstop research, reading drafts, editing, and mostly for the emotional support. And special thanks to Krystal, my trainer, who shared her own stories of dating and insights on men that were so relevant to this book. I appreciate Post Hill Press and my editor David Bernstein, for not only being willing to publish this book, but for showing enthusiasm for a topic that not many publishers would have the courage or interest to take on. Special thanks to my managing editor, Lauren Campbell, and to Barbara Pepe for copywriting and proofreading. And thank you to all the people around the country that I talked with in person and by Zoom who filled me in on what life is like for American men and boys.